Polly Day Van Lenten
920 Riverview Dr SE Apt 260
Rio Rancho, NM 87124-0958

D1490526

SI-COLOGY 1O1

SI-COLOGY 101

TALES & WISDOM FROM
DUCK DYNASTY'S
FAVORITE UNCLE

Si Robertson
with Mark Schlabach

SIMON & SCHUSTER

London · New York · Sydney · Toronto · New Delhi

A CBS COMPANY

First published in Great Britain by Simon & Schuster UK Ltd, 2013
A CBS COMPANY

5 7 9 10 8 6 4

Simon & Schuster UK Ltd
1st Floor
222 Gray's Inn Road
London WC1X 8HB

www.simonandschuster.co.uk

Simon & Schuster Australia, Sydney
Simon & Schuster India, New Delhi

A CIP catalogue record for this book is available from the British Library

Designed by Davina Mock-Maniscalco

ISBN: 978-1-47113-371-8
eBook ISBN: 978-1-47113-372-5

Printed and bound by CPI Group (UK) Ltd, Croydon, CR0 4YY

Contents

Contents

SI-COLOGY 101

"You can't spell **squirrel without Si,** and that's me!"

PROLOGUE

MY PARENTS ABSOLUTELY RUINED me. One of the lessons they always preached was to tell the truth no matter what. The Bible says we should always be honest, and that's one of the virtues I've tried to live by. I grew up to be an honest man who always told the truth to my teachers, coaches, sergeants, and bosses. Hey, I was like George Washington—I could never tell a lie! I can't even cross my fingers behind my back, Jack!

I believe lying is a learned skill. Some people are good at it, while others aren't. I've always been a lousy liar. The key to being a good liar is to know when you can get away with it and when you can't. You have to keep a straight face if you're going to lie, and I could never stop smiling when I tried. My palms would get sweaty, and I'd lose my composure and start to stutter. Hey, I even grew a long beard so people couldn't call me a

Hey, I even grew a long beard so people couldn't call me a bald-faced liar.

bald-faced liar. Still, as much as I tried, I couldn't tell a lie!

My older brother Phil always told me that my nose would grow longer than Pinocchio's if I was ever dishonest, and I figured my nose was already big enough. Some people are great at lying. Poker players are great liars, and most politicians will never get elected if they can't lie. Hey, how do you know if a politician is lying? His lips are moving! Some great Americans were undone by not telling the truth: Bill Clinton, Richard Nixon, Lance Armstrong, Mark McGwire, the guys from Milli Vanilli, and Pete Rose, to name a few. I don't want to end up like them, so I always tell the truth. Hey, do you know what happens to a liar when he dies? He lies still, Jack!

My twenty-four years in the army would have been *much* easier if I'd told only a couple of white lies. I got myself into so much trouble in the military by simply telling the truth. I was passed over for promotions and given crummy assignments because I was always honest. If I'd told a few little lies, I might have left the army as a four-star general!

Well, I'm always honest, so I have to tell you about the time I tried to tell a lie while I was in the army. Hey, even the best of us slip up every once in a while! During my first year in Vietnam, I actually tried to lie to my commanding officer. I was extremely homesick and was desperately trying to get a furlough back to the United States. One day, I walked into my sergeant's tent.

"Sir, might I have a word with you?" I asked very politely.

"What is it, Private Robertson?" he said.

"Well, sir, my wife is extremely ill and the doctors can't figure out what's wrong with her," I said. "I really need to fly back to Louisiana to check on her. I think she might die."

"Robertson, I have some good news for you," he said. "We received a telegram this morning from your wife, and she's been released from the hospital. Everything's going to be fine. There's no reason for you to go home."

I scratched my head in disbelief.

"Sir, with all due respect, I have to tell you that we must be the two biggest liars in Vietnam," I said. "I don't even have a wife!"

Hey, if I've learned anything from being a part of *Duck Dynasty* it's that you can't believe everything you see or read. It always amazes me that if people see something on TV or read it on the Internet, they instantly believe it's true.

I remember going to church on a Sunday morning not long ago, and a little old lady walked up to me before the service started.

"Si, I'm so sorry about your vision," she said.

"Hey, what are you talking about?" I said. "My vision is perfect. It's forty/twenty!"

"No, you're blind, honey," she said. "I saw it on TV. It was on *Duck Dynasty*."

Hey, no matter what I told the lady, she thought I was blind! She even asked me if I needed to be escorted to a pew!

When Phil and I were making an appearance last summer, a pretty lady walked up to our table and said, "Here I am."

"Who are you?" I asked.

"I'm the lady that just drove three hundred and fifty miles to marry you," she said. "I'm ready. Let's go."

"Well . . . that's an interesting proposal, but there's someone I know who might object."

"Who's that?" she asked.

"Hey, I'm sorry, darlin'," I said, "but I've been happily married for more than forty years. I don't think my wife would like it if I got hitched to you, too."

"You mean I drove all this way for *nothing*?" she said. "Would you at least sign these T-shirts?"

Hey, you wouldn't believe the number of marriage proposals I get every week. Women send me letters, cards, e-mails, flowers, razors, and candy. For some reason, the women across America think I'm an eligible bachelor. Hey, sorry, ladies, I've been married since 1971!

It amazes me what people will say about you sometimes. A few months ago, the phone started ringing at my house one afternoon. All of my relatives and friends started calling me to make sure I wasn't dead! People were even calling Phil's house to make sure I was okay. Apparently, someone had advertised that I would be appearing at a festival in Louisiana. When a bunch of people showed up to see me and I wasn't there, one of the vendors at the festival told them that I'd been killed in a car wreck! Naturally, everybody thought I was dead. The news of my tragic demise spread like wildfire across the Internet! Hey, news flash, people: I'm still here!

As you read this book, there are a few things that you have to understand: 95 percent of my stories are truthful. Every member of the Robertson family has the God-given gift of storytelling. Hey, when you've sat in a duck blind for more than half of your life, you have to figure out some way to pass the time! It's better than looking at Willie and Jase for six hours! Many of the stories I like to tell happened when I was a young boy or when I was in Vietnam. My family members shared some of the stories over the dinner table, and other soldiers in Vietnam passed some of them on to me. At my age, a few of the details are cloudy, but I'll recollect the coming stories as best I can. Hey, just remember it isn't a lie if you think it's true! It's up to you, the reader, to figure out what's true and what's fiction. Best of luck with that, Jack! May the force be with you.

Hey, another thing you have to know: my stories are kind of like my vocabulary. You might have noticed I like to say "hey" quite a bit. "Hey" can mean anything. It can mean "yes," it can mean "maybe," and it can mean "no." Hey, it could mean "next week." The bottom line is, you have to understand "hey" to understand me.

And if you know anything about Silas Merritt Robertson, you know I'm a hard rascal to figure out.

"The naked truth is much better than the best-dressed lie."

Birthday Suit

LIKE EVERY OTHER HUMAN on earth, I came into this world in the buff. According to my brothers and sisters, I stayed that way throughout much of my early childhood. For whatever reason, I never liked to wear clothes when I was a boy, so I ran around our farm buck nekkid. I guess I figured since God brought me into this world in my birthday suit, I might as well wear it. Hey, some people have it, and some people don't. I've always had it, Jack!

When I was born on April 27, 1948, my parents, Merritt and James Robertson, were living in a log cabin outside of Vivian, Louisiana. The cabin was really rustic; we used an outhouse and didn't even have hot water to take baths. I was the youngest of five sons: Jimmy Frank was the oldest boy, followed by Harold, Tommy, and Phil. I had an older sister, Judy, and then my younger sister, Jan, came along a few years after I was born.

Our log cabin sat on top of a hill and was surrounded by about four hundred acres. Marvin and Irene Hobbs, Momma's brother-in-law and sister, lived at the bottom of the hill. They had several kids: Billy, Mack, Sally, and Darrell, who were our first cousins. When Momma and Daddy played dominoes at the Hobbses' house, Jimmy Frank was put in charge of the younger kids. Our cabin became a prison, and Jimmy Frank was the warden. He'd walk outside the cabin, as if on patrol, making sure none of the younger kids escaped, so we always called him the warden! We younger kids wanted to go to the Hobbses' house to play with our cousins, but Jimmy Frank was under strict orders to keep us inside.

There were only two windows in the cabin, and they were our routes of escape. As the warden marched around the log cabin, one of us captives would watch him through the cracks in the walls. When he made his way around the right corner of the house, we'd all jump through the window and run down to the Hobbses' place. At least there weren't any sirens when we made our getaway!

My daddy started working in the oil industry when he was young, first as a roughneck, then as a driller and tool pusher, and eventually he became a drilling superintendent. It was really hard work, but I never heard him complain about it. It was an honest living, and even though we never had a lot of money, we always had enough food to eat, which mostly came from the fields and gardens on our farm. And with so many kids around, we were never bored and always seemed to find something to keep us busy.

When I was a little bit older, we left the log cabin and moved to Dixie, Louisiana, which is about fourteen miles north of Shreveport. We made the move because Momma suffered a nervous breakdown and was diagnosed as manic-depressive. Living in Dixie made it easier for her to get the treatment she needed; she spent a lot of time in hospitals and the state mental institution. I loved my momma dearly, and my brothers and sisters always say I was her favorite child. Hey, what can I say? I've always had that effect on women!

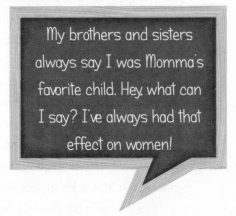

My brothers and sisters always say I was Momma's favorite child. Hey, what can I say? I've always had that effect on women!

A lot of my fondest childhood memories occurred in Dixie. I can still remember the day we drove to our house for the first time. We unloaded out of a 1957 Chevrolet and a couple of kids from the neighborhood walked up. We introduced ourselves to the boys, and the only way I can describe them is, well, they were geeks. We wandered around the yard, exploring the place, and noticed a big patch of woods about two miles from the railroad tracks in front of our house. We asked the boys, "Hey, what's over there?"

"We have no idea," they told us.

"What do you mean you have no idea?" I asked them. "Have you not been over there?"

"No, we've never been over there," one of them said.

The next thing they knew, Tommy, Phil, and I were racing across the railroad tracks and into the woods. We drove the farmers around our house slap insane by hunting on their land without permission. One of the farmers loved to chase us out of the woods in his pickup truck. Every time we heard his pickup coming, we'd take off running like deer through the woods. We hid behind logs and in underbrush, looking for his truck at the top of a hill or in the pecan orchard. It was like Wile E. Coyote chasing the Road Runner. He never did catch us.

Years later, we found out that chasing us was one of the farmer's favorite things to do. Momma sold Avon cosmetics for a while, and one day she was at the farmer's house selling products to his wife. Momma apologized to the farmer for our hunting on his land, but he told her we were allowed to hunt on any of his property. Momma thanked him and was getting ready to walk out the door.

"Hey, wait a minute," he said. "Don't tell them."

"Well, you gave them permission," she said.

"Oh, yeah, they can hunt on all of my land whenever they want," he said. "But don't tell them I gave them permission. If they know they have my permission, they won't run from me."

That farmer loved the chase. We ran from him for about fifteen years and didn't even have to!

Phil, Tommy, and I were always hunting or fishing. One of the best things we did happened when the sun went down. When Phil was ten years old, he got an air rifle for Christmas. I was eight and got a Daisy BB gun. We spent every day going around the neighborhood, shooting anything we could kill. When the sun went down, we got our flashlights and shined them under the awnings over the windows of our neighbors' houses. Birds loved to fly up there and go to sleep. Guess what? We loved to shine our flashlights on the birds and shoot them! Every night, our neighbors would be awakened by the *clank! clank! clank!* sounds.

Imagine their surprise when they opened the curtains and saw a bare-bottomed gunman!

"I like a dog that fits my personality: well-groomed, handsome, a natural-born killer, **and one that doesn't** mind taking a nap **once in a while."**

Chapter 2

Dynamic Dog Duo

MARK TWAIN ONCE SAID the difference between a cat and a lie is that a cat only has nine lives. Hey, let me tell you something: where I grew up, cats didn't have nine lives—they generally had just one! There weren't many second chances when the Robertsons were involved!

We always had a lot of animals around our house, whether it was chickens, cows, pigs, rabbits, or horses, but I had two favorite family pets. Maimey was a Wiedemeyer—or a Weimaraner as they call them—and she was a good hunting dog. Bullet was a cur, a Louisiana Catahoula leopard dog, which is a fancy way of saying she was a mutt. The breed is actually named after Catahoula Parish on the Ouachita River, which runs in front of the house where Phil and Kay live today.

The Catahoulas are believed to be the first dogs bred in

North America; some people even suspect that Native Americans bred their dogs with the molossers and greyhounds that Hernando de Soto brought to Louisiana in the sixteenth century. Curs really aren't true hounds, but they're great hunting dogs and terrific at tracking wild boar. Many of them have spotted coats, and nearly all of them have distinctive marbled glass eyes. Bullet had one glass eye and a black and yellow coat. We always knew our toast was perfect when it was the color of Bullet's coat.

I remember the day Bullet died. A truck hit him on the road in front of our house. Phil and I saw it and were crying as we climbed onto the school bus. By the time we got to school, everybody on the bus was crying and then everybody in our class was crying. All the kids knew Bullet because they were always hanging out at our house.

Maimey was a much bigger dog than Bullet and had a slick silver coat. Now, one of the problems with the Weimaraner breed is that the dogs are typically stubborn and not very smart. But Maimey was quite the exception. Not only would she listen to our commands, she would even talk to us on occasion!

In fact, Maimey was Momma's alarm clock when we were young. Every morning, Momma would wake up early to cook us breakfast before we left for school. While Momma was cooking eggs, bacon, and buttermilk biscuits, she talked to our dogs.

"How are you this morning?" she would ask them. "Are you having a good day?"

Even though none of us believed her, Momma insisted the dogs talked back to her.

When it was time for us to wake up for breakfast, Momma would send Maimey to our room.

"Okay, wake them up," Momma told her.

Maimey liked to leap into our beds and put her cold, wet nose on our faces to wake us. Once she received Momma's command, she'd take off running around the corner in the kitchen and then sprint down the long hall to our beds. Most of the time, we heard Maimey's claws scratching the hardwood floors before she jumped on our beds. This was our fair warning to pull the quilts over our heads. Our house was always cold in the winter—there were only a few floor heaters scattered through the shotgun house—and Maimey's nose was ice-cold after being outside. Once Maimey found an opening in the blankets, she'd root her way under them and there we were— jumping out of bed!

It was impossible to keep Maimey out of the house. When we tried to put her outside, she'd open the front door. I guess she learned to open it by watching us turn the doorknob; she finally realized she could do it with her paws. When Maimey was ready to come inside, we'd hear scratching on the doorknob and then she'd waltz into the front room!

By the time we moved from the log cabin to our house in Dixie, Louisiana, Jimmy Frank and Harold were in school at Louisiana State University in Baton Rouge. One night, Tommy, Phil, and I were sitting at the dinner table with Pa and Granny (that's what we called my parents after their first grandchildren were born). It was one of the rare occasions when Maimey was outside.

As soon as we started eating dinner, the front door opened

and Maimey came running in. She looked at Momma and growled something I didn't understand.

"What did she say?" Momma asked us. "I think she just said, 'Harold is home.'"

Our dog Maimey looked at Momma and growled something I didn't understand.

A couple of minutes later, we heard a car door shut and then Harold walked in through the front door.

My brothers and I were dumbfounded. Nobody said anything as we looked at each other.

"Hey, I've been telling you I talk to her all the time," Momma told us. "And she talks back to me."

Finally, I believed her.

When Daddy worked as a driller, he was on the graveyard shift and some of his workers would occasionally come to our house before their shift. One night, one of our distant cousins, Wade Childs, was sitting in a dark green chair next to the fireplace. He didn't know it was Maimey's bed. Our front door was glass, so we could see through it from top to bottom. Wade was facing the door and saw the knob turning. Since it was nighttime, he couldn't see Maimey because of her dark coat.

Wade must have thought a ghost was opening the door. His eyes got bigger and bigger, and then Maimey walked through the door. She walked straight toward him and sat in front of the chair.

Then she started growling at him. She didn't bark; it was only a low growl in her throat.

"Merritt!" Wade screamed. "Merritt!"

Mamma walked in from the kitchen and asked him what was wrong.

"I didn't do anything," he said.

"Oh, you need to get out of her chair," Momma told him. "She's telling you she's ready to go to bed."

Wade got out of the chair, and Maimey jumped into it. She sneezed and spun around three times before taking a seat.

Before Maimey started to snore, I swear I heard her say, "Sleep tight and don't let the bedbugs bite."

Whenever we went hunting and fishing, Bullet and Maimey were always with us. They were great at retrieving ducks, doves, quails, squirrels, or whatever other game we were hunting. But Maimey had more of a thirst for blood.

Every morning when we went outside to wait for the school bus, Bullet and Maimey would sit and wait with us. Bullet would lie down on the ground, but Maimey would run across the railroad tracks in front of our house and into a big mess of dewberry bushes. She wouldn't be gone three minutes but always came back with a rabbit in her mouth. She did it every morning, Monday through Friday, without exception. Maimey would come back, lie down, eat the head off the rabbit, and leave the rest. Don't know why she didn't eat the body, but that's what she did. Every day when we came home from school, Momma would tell us to get the rabbit carcass off the front porch. I knew rabbits liked briar patches, but I couldn't believe how many rabbits were over there!

Bullet was named exactly right, because he was *fast*. He was like a cheetah chasing antelope running through the woods. Maimey was a bigger dog than Bullet and wasn't quite as swift. Together, though, they were the dynamic duo and the greatest cat-killing team I have ever seen.

Bullet was adept at getting in front of a cat and keeping its attention while Maimey would sneak up from behind and pounce. She would break its neck before she was ever clawed. Bullet was fast, but he wasn't as quick as a cat. There were several times he came home covered with cat scratches.

Our friend Tommy McKenzie's grandmother Mrs. Wilson lived next door to us in Dixie. Purple jasmine grew over the back door of her house. When it bloomed, it was beautiful and you could smell the flowers all the way from our house. Mrs. Wilson also had forty Siamese cats. Now, I'm not much of a cat person, but I have to admit her cats were something to look at. Their coats had different colors, and she spent a lot of time grooming them.

> When I left to join the army at nineteen. Mrs. Wilson had only two cats left! Bullet and Maimey killed nearly every one of them.

Hey, when I left to join the army at nineteen, Mrs. Wilson had only two cats left! Bullet and Maimey killed nearly every one of them. The lone survivors lived at the top of a big walnut tree in her backyard. The only time we saw those two cats was when we looked up the giant tree. The two cats were always sitting at the tip-top of it. Talk about survivors! Those cats knew that if their paws ever hit the ground, they'd be goners.

Out of Mrs. Wilson's forty cats, Maimey and Bullet killed thirty-eight of them! Mrs. Wilson would walk over and say to Momma, "I don't know what's happening to my cats. They keep disappearing."

Fortunately for us, Mrs. Wilson was about half deaf. Whenever anyone asked her about living next door to us, she always said, "Oh, they're the sweetest boys. They never make any noise. They're the quietest people you'd ever want to be around."

Hey, you know what they say: *See no evil, hear no evil, speak no evil!*

"Once I reached down
to pet a little dog and when I did,
it was a five-pound squirrel."

Redneck Pets

WHEN WE LIVED IN the log cabin near Vivian, Louisiana, there were two big hickory trees in the front yard. If you've cracked open a hickory nut before, you know there is a green nut inside. Once you crack the thick shell or it pops off once it's ripe, the nut is as hard as a brick! My brothers and I had wars throwing those things at each other, and they really hurt! If you were ever hit in the head, it left a goose egg on your noggin!

Until we were old enough to get a BB gun or some kind of firearm, we made slingshots and used the hickory nuts as ammunition. We'd take the inner tubes out of old tires and cut strips from them to use as slings. We found trees with forked limbs and tied the slings to the limbs with string. If you wanted a six-gun, you used a limb that was about six inches long. If you wanted to be like Wyatt Earp and have a long barrel, you made it twelve inches. Then we took the leather tongues out of old shoes and put the rocks and hickory nuts inside—for easy storage and carrying, ready to fire from the slings.

We killed plenty of game with the slingshots, from squirrels to rabbits to blackbirds. We also made our own bows and arrows before we had rifles. We used thick reeds as our arrows, sharpened them, and then tied broad rocks to them for arrowheads. Anything that walked or flew was fair game! Momma raised chickens at our house, and they were always running around our backyard. One day, Phil and I were messing around in the yard with our bows and arrows when one of Momma's chickens ran across the yard in front of us. Bad move, Jack! When the chicken made its way back to the other side, Phil fired an arrow and missed. On the second try, he hit the chicken right in the head.

Phil and I grabbed the dead chicken and went down to the creek that ran behind our house. We plucked the chicken, built a fire, and roasted it for lunch. We knew we had to eat the evidence before Momma found out! We never told Momma we killed her chicken, but she knew one of them was missing. She figured a fox or stray dog killed it.

Chickens weren't our only casualties. We used to hunt squirrels with our slingshots and bows and arrows—they've always been my favorite game to eat. But one time we found a baby squirrel that was still in its nest. Now, even I have a soft spot in my heart when it comes to young critters. We brought the baby squirrel home and fed it with an eyedropper. Somehow, the squirrel survived and became one of our pets. It crawled up on our shoulders and nibbled our ears every once in a while. Momma even allowed it to stay inside and roam around the house.

We managed to keep the squirrel until the day Momma

bought a new sofa for our living room. After we moved the sofa into our house, the squirrel crawled underneath it and wouldn't come out. It ate a hole through one of the boards and built a nest under the cushions. Every time someone sat on the sofa, a spring popped him in the butt because the squirrel had pulled out all of the cotton. I'd never seen my momma so mad! Needless to say, the squirrel was banished from the house and never allowed to come back.

Being rednecks, squirrels weren't our only exotic pets. One day, Momma sent Phil and me to the store to buy a gallon of milk. On our way, we saw a flock of pigeons sitting on the roof of a cotton gin. We looked around and found a handful of flat rocks—we called them sailers—to hurl at the pigeons. Sailers are the best rocks to throw; if you throw them on water, they're really good skippers.

"You throw first," I told Phil.

"Nah, you throw first," he said. "When you throw, they're going to jump up and then I'm going to get me one."

I wound my arm back like Nolan Ryan and fired a rock at the pigeons. I knew I was fixing to nail one because I'd found the perfect sailer. As the rock made its way toward the cotton gin, I could see the pigeons getting anxious and fidgety. As the rock started its descent, they got *really* nervous. It was like artillery falling from the sky. You know what they say about nuclear war: all pigeons are cremated equally! Just about the time the pigeons jumped up off the roof, my rock nailed one of them.

Phil and I ran to the cotton gin and picked the pigeon up off the ground. My rock had hit him squarely in the head and somehow twisted his head around. The pigeon was looking straight back! The rock snapped his neck, but he wasn't dead!

We had a pigeon coop at our house, so Phil and I carried the bird home, along with the gallon of milk. I put the pigeon in the coop, where it always sat on the top perch, his chest facing our house and his head looking behind him. I named the pigeon Eagle. Every morning, I went to the coop to pet Eagle and feed him. When I took Eagle out of the coop and threw him into the air to fly, he flew straight into the ground and rolled over. How can you fly if you can't see where you're going? Phil and I used to throw him up into the air just for the fun of watching poor Eagle.

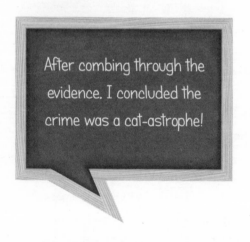

After combing through the evidence, I concluded the crime was a cat-astrophe!

Now, we found Eagle before Bullet and Maimey, our family dogs, ravaged Mrs. Wilson's prized collection of Siamese cats. One morning I woke up and went to the coop to feed our pigeons. As I walked down the hill, I was immediately struck with terror to see there had been a mass murder. There were blood and feathers everywhere in our pigeon coop! There were half-eaten carcasses lying on the floor.

I set out to solve the crime. It's obvious that you can't spell "NCIS" without "Si"—and that's me! After combing through the evidence, I concluded the crime was a cat-astrophe! Out of twenty-five pigeons, Mrs. Wilson's cats had killed every one—except Eagle!

Eagle was still sitting on the top perch, his chest facing me and his head looking the other way. The only thing I could figure was that the cats were superstitious and were afraid to kill him.

Or maybe Eagle had eyes in the back of his head and managed to fend for himself!

"When you were born
and they were handing out brains,
you thought they said 'trains.'"

Book Report

Aᴼᵀᴱᴿ ᴶᴵᴹᴹʸ FᴿᴬNK ᴬND Harold left for college, Tommy, Phil, and me went everywhere together. We were insepa-rable. I'm not sure Tommy and Phil wanted to drag their little brother everywhere they went, but Momma didn't give them much choice. If they were leaving to play football, going fishing or hunting, or going to town, Momma always told them, "Take little brother with you."

Tommy, Phil, and I were like stair steps everywhere we went. Tommy always walked in the front, and he was about four inches taller than Phil. I walked behind Phil, who was four inches taller than me. Since I was the youngest brother, I always brought up the rear.

When Momma would get tired of us, she'd load us up in our Ford Falcon and drive to Belcher, Louisiana, which was about ten miles from where we lived and was where we went to middle school. She'd drop us off at the Red River levee and say, "Go catch us a mess of fish; I don't want to see y'all until supper time."

Basically, Momma was letting us know that she was tired of us and needed a day off. Hey, if I spent most of my adult life around five boys, I'd need a vacation every once in a while, too!

When Momma dropped us off, we'd follow the river back toward our house. We'd usually float down the river on a log for about five miles, get off where the river started to make an S-curve around a bend, and then walk the last two or three miles to our house. We were always exploring that river, like we were in a Huckleberry Finn adventure.

If we were at the river, we were usually fishing. We used throw lines on the river, and it was a three-man operation. We used a brick and nylon rope with hooks. We could make the throw line however long we wanted to make it, as long as it was short enough for us to control. We usually went with twelve hooks on each throw line. We cut a thick branch off a willow tree, and drove it into the ground. Then we tied the throw line to the top and bottom of the branch. Before we were ready to fish, two people had to catch live brim and carry them in a washtub full of water.

One of us was in charge of throwing the brick and rope into the water, making sure not to hook ourselves in the process. After we hooked ourselves several times, we finally used our brains and learned to make the rope between the last hook and brick long enough so it wouldn't hook us. While one of us was throwing the brick into the water, somebody else had to hold the rope at the willow branch, making sure the throw line didn't slap the water and knock the bait off the hooks. The third person was in charge of making sure each of the twelve hooks always had fresh bait on it.

Usually, we set out four or five throw lines on the river at once, so we'd have as many as sixty hooks in the river at the same time. Let me tell you something: there's not a finer sight than seeing a willow branch shaking back and forth because there are so many fish on your throw line. We used to get so excited running to the lines, pulling in fifteen-pound blue catfish. We also caught Opelousas catfish and high-fin blue catfish. We'd come home with three washtubs full of catfish. It was fish-fry time! The whole neighborhood would come over to eat when they smelled the grease at the Robertson house.

> There's not a finer sight than seeing a willow branch shaking back and forth because there are so many fish on your throw line.

We supplemented whatever Momma and Daddy bought at the grocery store with catfish, crappie, white perch, and the game we killed in the woods.

Our fishing trips became legendary among our friends. During high school, we were required to read a book, write a book report, and then stand in front of the entire class and give an oral report on what we read. I was prepared to give a report on *The Adventures of Tom Sawyer*. But when I stood up in front of my class, one of the other students said, "No, no! We've already read *Tom Sawyer*. We know Si and Phil skipped school last Thursday. We want to know what they did last Thursday!"

I looked at my teacher, Mrs. Jones, and asked, "Well, what do you think?"

"Tell them what you did last Thursday," she said. "But know this: it better be good, because I am grading you on this."

So I proceeded to tell my class what I did the previous Thursday.

Momma woke up early like always last Thursday and fixed us a good breakfast. But then she changed her mind and decided Phil and me weren't going to school.

"I'm hungry for fish," she told us. "I want y'all to go catch me a mess of crappie."

Phil and I started jumping up and down. Any day at the lake was better than spending a day at school. So Phil and I sat in the front room of our house, looking out the window for the school bus with our noses just above the windowsill. The bus stopped right between the shrubs in front of our house, and the bus driver opened the door and then blew the horn. Momma walked out and waved her on.

Phil and I gave the bus driver just enough time to turn left at the end of our street, and then we ran out the back door to get our cane poles, washtubs, and bait. We jumped in the Falcon and drove fifteen miles to an oxbow lake on the Red River. We climbed into a boat that the man who owned the lake allowed us to use, and we were ready to catch some crappie.

But when we got out on the lake, there was a north wind of about thirty miles per hour. It was a bad day to be fishing on open water. The lake had once been a channel of the Red River, but now it was landlocked and there were no trees to block the wind. It was wide open, and we were paddling against winds of thirty miles per hour.

When we finally reached our favorite spot to fish, Phil and I realized a commercial fisherman had recently been there. We saw two sticks in the water, about one hundred and fifty yards apart, and we knew that was where he'd tied off his net. Phil and I threw our lines into the water right there, and as soon as our shiners hit the water, we each caught a pound-and-a-half crappie. By the time we had the fish in our boat, we were one hundred and fifty yards away from the sweet hole. So we paddled against thirty-mile-per-hour winds again, and then dropped our lines in the water and caught another fish. We looked up and we were one hundred and fifty yards away from the sweet spot again!

Finally, after about the third time of doing this, Phil said, "Hey, this isn't going to work. One of us is going to have to paddle to keep us here while the other one fishes."

Of course, I was the youngest, so I became a three-and-a-half-horsepower human trolling motor to keep Phil between the sticks.

Phil sat there and caught about seventy-one more crappie. We ended up with seventy-five crappies in our boat and then had one heck of a fish fry that night.

After I finished telling the story, all of the kids in my class clapped. One of my buddies said, "That's what I'm talking about."

I stood up from my chair and looked at my teacher. "C-minus," she said.

"C-minus?" I asked her. "Have you lost your mind? Seventy-five white perch in thirty-mile-per-hour winds, and I was the motor! You're giving me a C-minus?"

She looked at me and shook her head.

"Hey, woman," I said. "I've got a news flash for you: That is an A-plus!"

"Hey, fear is a healthy thang."

Unidentified
Walking Object

THERE ARE ONLY A few things in this world I fear: poisonous snakes, losing my iced tea cup, not being able to take
a nap, and being left alone in the dark. Hey, I'm man enough to
admit that I'm afraid of the dark. I like the world better when it's
light outside; you can see what's in front of you or, more important,
what's lurking behind you. I'm not actually afraid of the dark—I'm
scared of what's in it, Jack!

I'm not exactly sure when I was diagnosed with achluopho-
bia—the fear of darkness—but I've always been afraid to be left
alone in the dark. Growing up in the Robertson house, my older
brothers always teased me about being scared of the dark. I spent
many nights in bed with the covers pulled over my head while
Tommy and Phil tapped on the walls or made scary noises to
frighten me. I don't like to watch horror movies and didn't even

like to go trick-or-treating when I was a kid, unless we were back at our house before the sun went down! I always checked to make sure the doors and windows were locked—and the closets were clear—before I went to bed, and I even slept with a nightlight until I left for Vietnam. Now I sleep with the TV on in our bedroom. I still don't like the dark!

Whenever we went fishing or frog gigging at night when we were kids, Tommy and Phil liked to run off and leave me alone in the woods. I always feared that a grizzly bear, Sasquatch, or a fifty-pound squirrel was going to eat me. Hey, you probably didn't know squirrels could grow that big, but I've seen them! They have razor-sharp teeth and don't look anything like the cute squirrels that eat nuts. They're man-eaters and like to gnaw on human bones! They'd probably like nothing more than to eat the hunters who are trying to shoot them, including me!

I've been afraid of the dark for as long as I can remember. One night, Momma asked me to go outside to get her shoes, which she'd left on the front steps of our log cabin.

"Momma, I don't want to go outside," I told her. "It's dark out there."

Momma smiled and said, "Silas, you don't have to be afraid of the dark, son. Jesus is out there. He'll watch over you and protect you."

"Are you sure he's out there?" I asked her.

"Yes, Silas, he's always with you," she said.

So I mustered up the courage to crack open the front door. I stuck my head outside. It was pitch-black, and I could hear the grizzly bears and fifty-pound squirrels stirring in the woods around our house.

"Jesus?" I asked, while praying he would respond to my plea. "If you're out there, can you hand me Momma's shoes?"

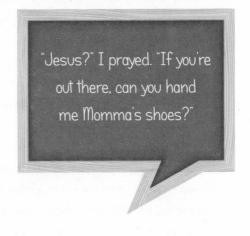

"Jesus?" I prayed. "If you're out there, can you hand me Momma's shoes?"

Well, Jesus never handed me her shoes, so I'm still afraid of the dark.

Momma always told me my fear of darkness would go away once I got older, but it only seemed to get worse over the years. When I was in the fourth grade, Tommy, Phil, and I went frog gigging one night. After we'd gigged a bagful of bullfrogs, we started to make our way through the dark woods back to our house to clean them. We were walking in a straight line, like we always did, with Tommy in the front and Phil in front of me.

As we were walking through the woods, I kept hearing something walking behind me. Tommy had the flashlight, so I was trying to make sure that I kept Phil in sight. I didn't want to be left alone out there! No matter how fast I walked, I kept hearing footsteps behind me. After I heard the footsteps once more, I turned around and looked but didn't see anything. I figured I was only imagining the sounds because it was so dark in the woods and, hey, I was scared.

The next time I turned around, though, I saw a pair of yellow eyes looking right at me! The eyes were glowing in the dark!

I tried to muster up enough courage to scream, but my mouth

was as dry as the Sahara Desert. I sat there in the woods, shaking and trembling in my boots, wondering what was about to eat me for dinner. Suddenly, I remembered a Bible verse Momma read to me. It was Isaiah 41:10:

> So do not fear, for I am with you; do not be dismayed,
> for I am your God. I will strengthen you and help you;
> I will uphold you with my righteous right hand.

I reached out for God's right hand but couldn't find it. So I looked for the next-best thing: Phil's shoulders! I took off running and ran right into Phil's back, and then he fell into Tommy. We fell into a clump on the ground.

"Hey, hey!" Tommy yelled. "Si, what's going on?"

"There's something behind me!" I screamed. "It's Sasquatch!"

Tommy shined the flashlight back to where I'd seen the unidentified walking object. We didn't see anything.

"You're imagining things," Phil told me. "You're such a sissy."

But when Tommy shined the light back to the spot again, we saw a big blur run past us. It jumped into a large culvert to our left.

"I told you there was something back there!" I said.

We slowly tippytoed toward the culvert and shined the light down into it. We didn't see anything, but we were suddenly overcome by the putrid scent of a skunk. It smelled awful.

"Si, it was only a skunk," Phil said.

To this day, Tommy and Phil still contend I only saw a very large skunk.

Hey, I don't know about you, but I've never seen a skunk that walks upright and is four feet tall! Even now, I still have no idea what the unidentified walking object really was. It had eyes that glowed in the dark and walked just like we do. It fell in line right behind us as we walked through the woods!

Maybe it was a four-foot skunk. We grow them pretty big down in Louisiana. Or maybe it really was Sasquatch and he badly needed a bath!

"He's like a snake in the grass.
Hey, if you chop its head off,
It'll still bite ya!"

Chapter 6

Snake Bit

ONE OF THE BIGGEST hazards of living in Louisiana is that nearly forty different species of snakes are here. Where I live, snakes hide under rocks, logs, floor mats, and pillows. Hey, they even sleep in your boots! If you're not careful, they'll crawl into your pocket when you're walking to the duck blind and back. Heck, I have to check my gun barrel every time I shoot to make sure a snake didn't crawl into it. As you may can guess, I don't like snakes. The only good snake is a dead snake! If anyone tries to mess with me when it comes to snakes, they're going to have a fight on their hands.

Given as much time as I've spent in the woods hunting squirrels, birds, deer, and other game, along with being on the water fishing and shooting ducks, the odds were pretty good I was going to be bitten by a snake. In fact, I've been bitten by a snake twenty-seven times in my life, to be exact. Over the years, water snakes, pine snakes, blind snakes, brown snakes, garter snakes, ribbon snakes, rat snakes, racers, and king snakes have bitten me. Hey, I don't blame the snakes. That's what a snake does—they're snakes!

Looking back, it's amazing that a poisonous snake never bit my brothers or me. I guess Momma was right; someone was always watching over us. Northwest Louisiana, where we grew up, is one of the few places in the United States that is home to all four of the venomous snakes of North America: the copperhead, cottonmouth, coral snake, and rattlesnake. We're even blessed to have two kinds of rattlesnakes: the canebrake and the eastern diamondback. Boy, aren't we lucky?

You always have to be on the lookout for snakes. You never know when one is going to be lying in the path of your next step as you're walking through the woods or swamp. Fortunately, Phil detests snakes as much as I do, so there are always two sets of eyes scanning the ground for them.

My brothers and I had plenty of close calls when we were kids. One day, while we were running on a sandbar on the Red River, Tommy stopped dead in his tracks. What followed next was like something out of a cartoon. Phil bumped into Tommy, and I ran into Phil's back. It was like dominoes falling over. We landed about six inches from a big snake.

"Whoa, whoa!" Tommy screamed. "It's a king cobra!"

We looked down and saw a big black snake on the ground. It was standing on its tail with its head flared up. The king cobra was staring straight at us and looked ready to strike and send us to our graves.

We stepped back and the snake backed down. It coiled up on the ground, and its head returned to normal.

"Nah, I've seen a picture of one of these snakes in a book at school," Tommy said. "It's not a king cobra snake. It's a hognose snake."

Since it wasn't a king cobra that could kill us with one strike, Tommy caught the snake with his bare hands. It kept flaring its head at us while we played with it. It was a bad-looking thing! When it calmed down, its head looked like it had a pig's nose with big nostrils. But when it flared up, it was wicked-looking!

One summer, we learned we could sell dewberries for about five dollars per gallon bucket, so we went into high gear gathering them. We went anywhere to find them. Dewberries are closely related to blackberries and raspberries, but they're bigger and grow on trailing vines that look like weeds. We sold them to women who used them to make cobblers, jams, or pies. We always saved enough for Momma to jar or turn into a Sunday cobbler. Five dollars a bucket was a lot of money for boys who never had much money in their pockets, so we searched for them day and night. We kicked it into high gear, Jack, and we went to picking dewberries fast and furious.

After a few weeks, we tapped out our sweet holes, so we went searching for more brambles of dewberries. We walked down the levee at the Red River, looking for dewberries along the bank. At the bottom of the incline, Tommy spotted some dewberries.

"Hey, we have to get down there," Tommy told us. "If there are dewberries down there, they're going to be big because they're close to the water."

Sure enough, we found some dewberries. We were on one knee wading through the water, picking dewberries at the edge of the river. They were as big as fifty-cent pieces! I was counting the money we were going to make in my head. Phil and I filled our buckets in about three minutes.

When Phil and I were finished, we walked back to the top of the levee, which was about six feet above the water at a forty-five-degree incline. Phil looked down at Tommy, who was still on one knee. Right above him on the bank were two big black rings with a white spot in the middle of them. The rings were four inches from Tommy's leg. It was two cottonmouth water moccasins, which are some of the meanest and deadliest snakes you'll come across. The snakes were about as big as my arm, about four inches in diameter. They looked like they could kill an eight-hundred-pound bull!

"Tommy, look down at your right knee!" Phil yelled.

I heard Tommy scream, and then the next thing I knew, Tommy was standing between Phil and me! Both of our mouths just dropped open. He jumped six feet from the water to the top of the hill!

I never saw Tommy run up the hill. He was at the bottom of the hill and then he wasn't!

I never saw Tommy run up the hill. He was at the bottom of the hill and then he wasn't!

After catching our breath, we found big sticks and killed the two snakes.

"Hey, I've got to figure this out," Tommy said.

Tommy is smart and always has to have a logical reason for why something happens. He went back into the water where he was kneeling, jumped up, and ran up the hill. It took him about six seconds. He tried to jump out of the water, but he could only jump about three feet. Then he went to the top of the hill, ran down, and jumped, but it wasn't much farther. No matter how much Tommy tried, he couldn't duplicate the feat.

Now, I've read several stories about hysterical strength and how adrenaline allows humans to do things they normally couldn't do. In 2011, a University of South Florida football player named Danous Estenor lifted a 3,500-pound Cadillac Seville off a tow-truck driver who was pinned under its rear tire. In 2006, an Eskimo woman named Lydia Angiyou distracted a 705-pound polar bear long enough for hunters to arrive and rescue her seven-year-old son and two other children. And in 1982, a Georgia woman named Angela Cavallo lifted a 1964 Chevrolet Impala off her son after two jacks fell. Now, that's a muscle car!

I don't know what the Olympic record is for the standing broad jump, but my older brother broke it that day. Those two cottonmouth water moccasins put springs in his knees!

"You put camouflage on anything
and it automatically becomes cool."

Chapter

7

Floating Log

HEY, REMEMBER WHAT I said about snakes being everywhere in Louisiana? News flash: snakes aren't even the state reptiles of Louisiana! It's the alligator. If you're walking through a swamp, lake, or river and don't step on a snake, chances are you'll step on an alligator. Bad news, Jack! The alligator is one mean sucker and, hey, it's a cold-blooded animal. I've seen alligators that are twenty feet long and weigh more than one thousand pounds. They'll eat fish, rats, crabs, birds, beavers, muskrats, raccoons, ducks, deer, and Milo the family dog. In Vietnam, I once saw an alligator wipe out an entire village on the Dong Nai River. It wasn't a pretty sight. A snake's bite might kill you, but it sure beats getting locked in the jaws of death!

Alligators live to be about fifty years old in the wild, and there's a reason they've survived for so long. They're the baddest predators in the swamp! They'll go through nearly three thousand teeth killing their prey before they die. When one tooth falls out, another one grows in its place. Nothing else has the courage to mess with them. Hey, how many arms does an alligator have? It depends what it ate for dinner, Jack! There are nearly two million alligators living in Louisiana, and I suspect more than half of them reside in our duck holes.

I've been running from alligators since I was a young boy. Momma taught me early that I could become an alligator's appetizer if I wasn't careful. We've never really hunted alligators, because we don't like to mess with them, but we're always mindful that one might be lurking close by when we're in the duck blind. Some time ago, I decided I wanted a pair of alligator boots. But every time I killed an alligator, it wasn't wearing any shoes!

Alligators are about the only game we haven't hunted—unless we had to. We never had much money growing up, but Daddy always made sure we had ammunition and guns for hunting because we wouldn't have much meat to eat if we didn't kill game. There were two guns in our house for us to use: Daddy's Browning semiautomatic sixteen-gauge shotgun and a Remington .22 that belonged to our uncle Al Robertson, which somehow wound up in our house. It was a bolt-action with a seven-shot clip. During duck season, we always managed to find a second shotgun to use.

When duck season opened my sixth-grade year, Daddy went out and bought us a couple of boxes of shotgun shells, like he did at the start of every season. Phil was in the eighth grade and was fourteen years old. On opening day, we jumped in the Ford Falcon, and Phil drove us—without a driver's license—to the duck hole, which was about fifteen miles from our house at Horseshoe Lake in Gilliam, Louisiana. Horseshoe Lake was one of our favorite holes to hunt mallard ducks. There were a bunch of willow trees growing at one end of the lake, and when the water level was high enough, mallard ducks sat in the hole. Phil knew the river was high, so it was time to go shoot mallard ducks.

"Let's go whack 'em," Phil said.

While we always had shotgun shells and guns to use, we were too poor to buy waders, which keep you dry when you're walking through the swamp to get to the duck hole. Blue jeans and tennis shoes were our waders! That's what we wore to wade through chilly water, regardless of what time of year it was. Hey, what do you get when you throw blue jeans and tennis shoes into a lake? A wet suit, Jack, and it made for some long days in the water!

What do you get when you throw blue jeans and tennis shoes into a lake? A wet suit, Jack!

When we arrived at Horseshoe Lake, we started to wade through the swamp. The water was about waist-deep, and it was early January, so the water was probably only twenty degrees. It was cold! After a few steps, Phil noticed a log sitting to the left of us.

"Hey, watch out," he told me. "Don't trip over that log."

I walked past the log and didn't think much of it.

After we found a spot in the duck hole that would conceal us—this was long before we started building duck blinds—we stood shaking in the water and waiting for the ducks. Fortunately, we had to wait only a few minutes before a flock of mallards came into sight. Phil called them over and they sailed right over us.

Boom! Boom! Boom! Boom!

We knocked down four mallard ducks, two apiece, on the first pass. Being the youngest brother, I waded through the ice-cold water and retrieved our kill. On my way back to the blind, Phil reminded me not to trip over the log.

"Hey, watch it," Phil said. "There's that log again."

"I see it," I said. "I'm not blind."

After a few more minutes, another bunch of mallards came into view. We both had guns, so we had three shots apiece. Phil called the ducks—he was really good at doing it even when he was young—and they flew right over our blind again. We each brought down three more ducks.

"Hey, there's a cripple over there," Phil said. "Shoot it again."

I looked to my left and there was a big mallard drake floating in the water by the log. He was still moving. I was closest to the wounded duck, so I aimed to shoot him again. But then I saw that the duck was facedown in the water, so I figured he was close to dying, so I wasn't going to waste another shell on him.

"Shoot him!" Phil yelled.

"Hey, he's dead," I said.

"No, he's not," Phil said. "Shoot him again!"

"Hey, trust me, he's deader than a lobster in butter sauce," I said. "I'm five feet from him. He's not going anywhere!"

That duck was spinning in the lake like water does when you're draining a bathtub. All of the sudden, the duck started spinning faster and faster. And then the big mallard drake was gone! It popped under the water like a cork does when you hook a two-pound crappie.

Floating Log

Then that twenty-foot log started moving! It sucked the mallard drake about two feet under the water! I looked at Phil and said, "Whoa, that log is an alligator!" We'd been walking around that stupid thing for thirty minutes!

Hey, news flash: we didn't walk on water that day, but we got out of it!

See ya later, alligator!

"I'm the master of distractions!
A couple of hand gestures and—*bam!*—
I'll pull the underwear clean off your butt!"

Chapter 8

Dancing with Wolves

YOU'VE GOT TO UNDERSTAND one thing about me: I had four older brothers and one older sister. I was the baby boy of the Robertson family. All of my life, wherever I went, people were always comparing me to my older siblings. If I did something wrong in school, one of the teachers would undoubtedly say, "Well, good grief, Harold wouldn't have done that." If I did something foolish at church, my Sunday school teacher might say, "Well, goodness, Si, Judy wouldn't have done that."

Hey, news flash: I'm not Harold and I'm not Judy! I'm Silas Merritt Robertson! Growing up, I had an identity crisis because I was always being compared to someone else. All of my life, all I ever heard was "You're not doing it like so-and-so used to do it." Hey, guess what? I'm not so-and-so! I'm me!

My older brothers are the reason I'm afraid of the dark and

still have separation anxiety to this day. We'd go into the woods to hunt or play hide-and-seek, and they'd run back to our house without telling me. They'd leave me in the woods alone, and they especially liked to pull the trick when it was dark. I would cry, "Hey, where did y'all go? Hey, come back! Please come back!" But even when it was light outside, I didn't like to be left alone. Hey, would you want to be left alone with the thoughts being pondered in this head? My mind, it's wide open. It's like a hollow tunnel of air!

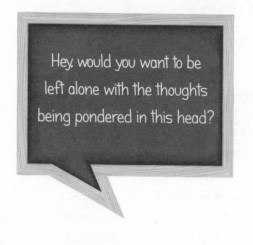

Hey, would you want to be left alone with the thoughts being pondered in this head?

When Phil was in high school, he came home one Friday and said he and a couple of his football teammates were going camping on the Red River. They were going to go fishing the entire weekend and wouldn't be home until Sunday. Of course, the first thing out of Momma's mouth was, "Take your younger brother with you." Andy Yarbrough and another football player came by our house to pick up Phil and me, and they made me ride in the back, while the three of them planned our trip in the cab.

They decided I was going to drive our boat across the Red River to a camping site on the other side and wait for them to get there. We pulled up to the Red River and put our boat in the water, and then they showed me how to crank the motor.

"You see that big log on the riverbank over there?" Phil asked me. "Drive the boat over there, tie it up good, and don't let it get away. We're going to drive the truck the long way, go across the bridge, and come in the back way to the woods. When you get to the other side, you'll see a trail. Follow it up the hill and you'll find the campsite. We'll see you in a little while."

"How long before you get there?" I asked him.

"We'll get there before dark," Phil said.

I told him as long as they were there before dark, I'd do it. I was in the ninth grade and was still afraid of the dark!

They left in the truck, and I motored the boat across the river just as the sun was starting to set. I parked the boat, tied it down, and then walked down the trail Phil told me about. I walked into the woods and quickly realized there wasn't a house or another human being within forty miles of me. I was in the wilderness. I had no idea where I was, but I somehow found the campsite, which was about a fifteen-foot circle slap in the very middle of the woods.

I sat down and waited for Phil and his buddies to get there. After about twenty minutes, I noticed the sun was going down over the horizon. It was barely visible. Darkness was coming—and it was coming quickly! I was getting more nervous with every passing second.

Suddenly I heard a ruckus behind me. It was a pack of wild wolves! Along with being terrified of the dark, I was also afraid of wolves. They were actually coyotes, but we called them wolves. When you have wild dogs that are capable of dragging down large cattle and killing full-grown bulls, they are *wolves*.

I was trying to keep my composure, but the sounds of the wolves were getting closer and closer. I stood up and looked behind me, and I saw one of the wolves poke its head out of the brush! It was looking right at me! I looked to my right and saw tire tracks going up the other side of the woods. As I pondered what to do, I saw another wolf stick his head out of the brush and then another one. I knew I was in trouble, so I took off running down the barely visible road. Hey, Fred Astaire's got nothing on me, but I wasn't about to be dancing with wolves! After I took off running, the wolves jumped in behind me and were yelping. They were getting louder and louder. I knew there were a bunch of them behind me but I was too afraid to look back. I felt like Little Red Riding Hood running through the woods to Grandmother's house!

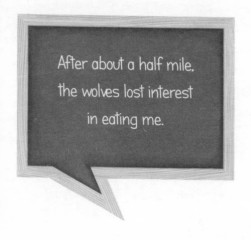

After about a half mile, the wolves lost interest in eating me.

I was running in second gear and my legs were already burning. But I knew if I slowed down, they were going to catch me. I shifted to third gear and thought, *Goodness, I've never run this fast!* But the wolves were gaining on me, and I could almost smell them when the road turned from dirt to gravel. The wolves were getting even closer, so I switched it to fourth gear. Then the dirt road switched to pavement, and I figured I'd better run with whatever I had left in my tank. So I put the pedal to the metal and sprinted at full throttle. I put the hammer down and was running in fifth gear!

After about half a mile, the wolves started losing ground, and then they lost interest in eating me altogether. If someone had timed me with a stopwatch, I would have set every world record from forty yards to ten miles! From a sprint to a marathon, I was moving, Jack!

Dancing with Wolves

When I stopped running, I bent over and tried to catch my breath. My lungs were burning and my shirt was drenched in sweat. *Good grief, it's hot,* I thought. Then I smelled burning rubber. I figured some farmer was using tires to start a brush fire.

But then I looked down, and the rubber soles of the tennis shoes I was wearing were on fire. They were ablaze in flames!

Fortunately, it had rained the night before, so I stepped into a mud puddle and extinguished both of my shoes before my feet were badly burned.

Hey, where there's smoke, there's fire, and I wasn't going to stick around just to be burned—or eaten!

"I sting like a butterfly
and punch like a flea!"

Chapter
9

Bumblebees

WHILE I WAS GROWING up, my favorite thing to eat for breakfast during the winter was Momma's homemade buttermilk biscuits with honey. Boy, were they good! It's hard for me to get much sweeter, but I just love the pure taste of honey. Now my wife tells me all the time, "I need honey, honey." Look, when you get honey in your beard, it literally stays there for two weeks. When my wife kisses me, she's like, "Oh, that was good." She doesn't even know why. She just thinks I'm sweeter than most males.

When I was seven, I was sitting on our front porch one day with Phil and Daddy. We looked over at Mrs. Wilson's house next door and saw a swarm of bees that had flocked on the purple jasmine over her back door. The swarm of bees was as big around as two basketballs.

"Hey, we're fixing to have us a beehive," Daddy said.

He told Phil and me to get two chairs out of the kitchen while he went to get a hammer. We walked into the backyard, where we had a one-room shed. Daddy took the hammer and knocked a knot out of a pine board on the side of the shed. Then he took a saw and cut a board out of the shed. He cut two two-by-fours and nailed them to the inside of the shed, which is where the bees could build a honeycomb. He nailed a board back on the shed, which could easily be taken off and put back on to get access to the beehive whenever we wanted.

"Get one of those chairs and come with me," he told us.

We walked over to the purple jasmine and put the chair in front of it. Daddy told me to stand on the chair.

"What do you mean get on the chair?" I asked him. "Those bees are fixing to tear me up."

"Boy, get up here on a chair before I take off my belt and tear you up," he said. "If you don't get up here, you're going to get torn up one way or the other."

I figured the bee stings wouldn't hurt as bad as Daddy's belt, so I climbed on the chair. Daddy cut one end of the vine with his pocketknife and handed it to me.

"Be careful," he said. "Don't be shaking the vine and moving it around or we will get stung."

Daddy cut the other end of the vine and told Phil to take the chair back to the shed and put it next to the other one. Then we carefully carried the vine with the hive hanging from it to the chairs. We slowly sat the vine on the chairs, with thousands of bees swarming around it. I didn't even know bees liked jasmine. I thought their favorite flowers were bee-gonias and honeysuckle! Hey, what do I know?

"Go get me another chair," Daddy said.

I brought him another chair, and he sat down and waited. Finally, the queen bee rolled up to the top of the vine, and Daddy flicked her into the hole in the shed. Within a matter of seconds, every one of the other bees followed her into the hole.

For the next ten years, whenever we wanted honey, we went to the shed, pulled the two nails out, and robbed the honeycomb.

One time when it was time to rob the beehive, Phil walked out wearing two pairs of blue jeans, three football jerseys, a pair of gloves, and a homemade screen-wire helmet that went down to his shoulders. Phil was convinced he couldn't be stung!

We didn't trust him, so Momma, Tommy, and me sat in the kitchen watching him through the window. Phil took the nails out and pulled out the board but didn't know there was a large honeycomb on the back of the board he had just pulled out! He threw it to the ground and it landed faceup! Within a matter of seconds, you couldn't see Phil's legs. They were covered in bees! He took off running, swatting the bees with every step. I don't know how many times he was stung, but it was a lot, Jack!

Whenever we robbed the honey, we cut out the honeycomb, leaving just enough for the bees to survive. By the time we were done squeezing the honeycomb, we'd have about three gallons of honey, which lasted for nearly a year. It was another way we lived off the land.

Phil wasn't the only one stung by bees. When Phil was in the eighth grade and I was in the sixth, we went squirrel hunting one day. As usual, Phil was walking in front of me, and we were about to cross under a barbed-wire fence. As Phil crawled under the fence, he grabbed ahold of a fence post, which was rotted from the ground up. As soon as he grabbed the post, bumblebees started swarming out of it. Phil took off running, but I was already making my way under the barbed wire before I noticed them. I panicked and unknowingly ripped my blue jeans clean across my rear. I took off running behind Phil, with the bumblebees chasing us.

As I was running, I remembered something Momma told me: if bees are chasing you, you're supposed to fall down and lie still, because they follow your vibration. So I fell down and played dead. Unfortunately, I didn't know my jeans were ripped. There was now a full moon in the middle of the day! I looked up and it was like World War II, with Allied fighter pilots bombing Germany. My white underwear was showing, and the leader of the bees said, "Boys, there's our target!" They must have had advanced targeting systems, because they didn't miss! Trust me, it didn't take them long to get me off the ground. I was running and crushing my underwear at the same time.

My white underwear was showing, and the leader of the bees said, "Boys, there's our target!"

When I got home, Momma said, "Well, drop your drawers." When I did, she busted out laughing.

"Hey, it's not funny," I said.

Bumblebees

"If you could see it from my angle, it's funny," she said. "That's the biggest your butt has ever been."

Momma sat in the kitchen and pulled twenty-seven bee stingers out of my rear while she and Phil laughed.

Look, what's worse than being a fool? Fooling with a bee, Jack! Like the Beatles sang, let it bee!

"Jack, I can hurt you,
physically and metaphysically."

Chapter
10

Kamikaze Pilot

WHEN PHIL LEFT TO play football with Tommy at Louisiana Tech University in Ruston in 1964, Jan and I were the only kids left in the house with Momma and Daddy. I was older than Jan, but I didn't pick on her because my older brothers picked on me so much. I didn't think it was the right thing to do, because she was a girl. If she had been a boy, I'm sure things would have been much different.

After Phil left for college, I still had to finish my junior and senior years at North Caddo High School in Vivian, Louisiana. I was a pretty good football player in high school, but there was this problem: I weighed one hundred and thirty-five pounds when I was soaking wet. If I had weighed one hundred and sixty or one hundred and eighty pounds, like Tommy and Phil, I would have gotten a scholarship to Louisiana Tech, there's no doubt in my mind.

We grew up playing football in our backyard. We even had goalposts at one end, which Jimmy Frank and Harold made from a couple of oak-tree uprights and a sweet-gum crossbar. Our football field was about thirty yards long and half as wide. We played two-hands-below-the-waist touch football year-round. Jimmy Frank managed to bring home a few old footballs from his high school team, so we were always playing in the backyard.

I played quarterback during my freshman and sophomore seasons at North Caddo High School and then moved to end on offense, and cornerback and linebacker on defense. Tommy and Phil were really good football players—they played quarterback and halfback and were all-district and all-state players—so I had a pretty big legacy to live up to. I wasn't very big, but I was crazy enough and dumb enough not to know that the guy I was trying to tackle was twice as big as me! I didn't care how big he was—I was coming in there like a torpedo! I was a kamikaze pilot on the football field. I was the meanest and craziest one-hundred-and-thirty-five-pound player on the field! Because my older brothers picked on me growing up, I didn't have a problem taking on guys who were bigger than me.

> I was crazy enough and dumb enough not to know that the guy I was trying to tackle was twice as big as me!

I really enjoyed playing football and probably got the most from my God-given abilities. I played in a couple of games as a senior in 1965, but then I broke my arm in a car accident and missed the rest of the season. When the season was over, my coach called me into his office and told me he could get me a try-out as a walk-on player at Louisiana Tech. He told me if I was good enough to make the team and worked hard to get bigger and stronger, the Louisiana Tech coaches might even be willing to give me a scholarship a couple of years down the road. My coach told me he thought I was talented enough to do it. When my coach was finished talking, I busted out laughing.

"Hey, I've been in the Louisiana Tech locker room with Phil and all those boys," I told him. "Excuse me, I've been in the locker room with Phil and all those *men*. I weigh one hundred and thirty-five pounds. I love the game, don't get me wrong, but I'm not stupid. I might not be the sharpest knife in the drawer, but I'm not the dullest one, either. I love football, but I'm not getting on the field with those men."

What I didn't tell my coach was that I wasn't even sure I wanted to go to college. I wasn't sure that four more years of school was the right thing for me. I'd had enough of going to class five days a week. Some parents get all bent out of shape because their kids don't want to go to college. Look, college isn't for every-one. I tried college ten times and never liked it. To me, college is an endurance test. You put up with four or five years of crap just for someone to hand you a piece of paper that says you have some sense.

Hey, news flash for all you people: I got sense without the paper! And I didn't have to endure four or five years of crap for someone to tell me I'm smart!

During the second half of my senior year of high school, we moved to Gonzales, Louisiana, because Daddy took a job there. I graduated from East Ascension High School in May 1966 with a bunch of strangers. It was terrible. Moving during my senior year really ruined my high school experience. I didn't get to graduate with the friends I grew up with, and we moved too late for me to make close friends with kids at my new school.

Right after high school, I went to work for Daddy as a welder's apprentice on an oil rig. It was grueling work. I did okay on the smaller rigs, but once we were on the bigger rigs, it was too much for me physically. I wasn't as strong as Phil and Tommy and didn't have their stamina. It didn't take me long to figure out that the off-shore drilling business wasn't for me.

A couple of months after high school ended, Momma informed me I was going to college, whether I wanted to go or not. While we never had much money, every one of my brothers and sisters graduated from college. Most of them even went back and received master's degrees.

"No, I don't want to go to college," I told Momma. "I don't want you and Daddy wasting your money."

"No, you're going to college," she said. "You don't have a choice."

"What don't you understand?" I asked her. "I'm going to go to college and do nothing but party."

Momma smiled at me and said, "Well, have a good one, because you're going to college."

I asked Momma why she wanted to waste her money on sending me to school.

"Because when you're out there digging ditches, I don't want you to say it was Mom and Dad's fault," she said. "We're giving you the opportunity to go to college."

Like it or not, it was up to me to make the most of it.

"I'm like an owl.
I don't give a hoot."

The roe deer in Germany aren't nearly as big as the white-tailed deer
we have in the United States, but they're just as tasty!

Chapter 11

C Is Always
the Best Answer

WHEN I ENROLLED AT Louisiana Tech in the fall of 1967, there were four Robertson brothers attending the same school. Tommy and Phil were playing on the football team, and Harold came there to get a master's degree after earning a bachelor's degree at Louisiana State University. It was like a family reunion.

While my older brothers were at Louisiana Tech to actually get an education, I went there for three quarters and did nothing but party for two of them. Hey, I told Momma that's what I was going to do, and I'm a man of my word!

I rarely went to class because I didn't have much interest in getting a college education. My partner in crime was Miss Kay's cousin Charles Hollier. We called him Tinker Bell, and he was flunking out of school, too. We pretty much had our own fraternity—Kappa Tappa Kegga. If I wasn't working at the mess hall or hunting and fishing with Phil and Tommy, I was drinking beer with Tinker Bell. He wasn't nearly as bad as I was about the partying. It didn't take me long to figure out there was always a party somewhere at college if you looked for it, and I usually took the time to find one!

We pretty much had our own fraternity— Kappa Tappa Kegga.

Every weekend, we had a get-together at either Tommy's house or Phil's. Both of them were married, so Miss Kay or Tommy's wife, Nancy, would cook us a big meal. They lived next to each other at the Vetville apartments, which the school built in 1945 to accommodate married veterans coming home from World War II. The red brick apartments were located on South Campus, about a mile from the main campus. Phil's front yard was always littered with fishing boats, motors, duck decoys, and on occasion, animal carcasses. His neighbors loved him!

During one gathering near the end of my third quarter at Louisiana Tech, Harold, Tommy, and Phil started getting on my case about not going to class. They were calling me stupid and lazy, and one of them said I wasn't smart enough to finish college.

"No, you're wrong there," I told them. "Being intelligent has nothing to do with this."

It's true that I was flunking out of school, and I'd only been there for a few months! I was already on double-secret probation with the dean as a freshman, and there wasn't much margin for error before I'd get thrown out of school. I really wasn't too worried about it. I made it to just enough classes so they couldn't kick me out of school for truancy, but I didn't expend much energy in studying for midterms and final exams.

With only a week to go in my third quarter, Tinker Bell came to me and asked me if I knew anyone who would give us the lecture notes for our classes.

"If I flunk out my daddy is going to kill me," Tinker Bell said.

"What do you think we can do about it now?" I asked him. "There's only a week until our finals, and we haven't been to class in a month."

"Hey, if you can get the notes, we'll hit the books," he said.

So I found a couple of girls who gave me copies of their notes from our classes. Hey, have you ever known a woman who could tell me no? Over the next four days, Tinker Bell and I studied seventy-four hours in a row. We never went to sleep! We went to the store and bought eight cases of soda pop. Look, I discovered that soda pop makes you drunk if you drink enough. This was back when they still used real sugar in sodas. We drank so many soda pops while studying that we were wired for four straight days. Hey, when we were done studying, I couldn't remember the last time I'd blinked! If someone had given me a cup of decaf coffee, I might have slipped into a coma! Thank goodness they hadn't invented Red Bull yet!

The day of my final exams, I did fine in my first three classes. I breezed through the final exams and was as alert as a one-legged man walking through a minefield in Vietnam. I was still wired from the caffeine. My last final exam was late in the afternoon and it was one of my least-favorite courses: Romance languages. Hey, what more could the professor have taught me that I didn't know already?

Look, the final exam was about one hundred questions. I answered about fifteen of them, and the next thing I knew the professor was shaking me! I fell asleep in the middle of the test!

"Wake up," he told me. "You don't have but ten minutes left to finish."

There was one thing in my favor: the test was multiple-choice! I didn't give a flip anyway, so I went through the answer sheet, filling in bubbles with my no. 2 pencil all the way down. The test sheet looked like an Etch A Sketch when I was done! Fortunately, I remembered that C is always a good answer! It took me only five of the ten minutes to complete the exam. I handed it to the professor and skipped out of the classroom.

I figured I had probably taken my last college exam, so I gave Tommy one hundred dollars to buy us some steaks. Phil and Tommy were going to grill steaks for us the next day at an end-of-the-quarter party at Tommy's house. I had a job in college, so I usually had a few more bucks than my brothers. I worked in the freezer department of the university's cafeteria. The cooks prepared turkeys and then sent them down to us to wrap and freeze. When the cooks were ready to serve the turkeys to students, they'd thaw them out and warm them up. One day, I went to work without eating lunch. Every time a turkey came down, I picked a little piece of meat off it. Hey, when you've picked forty turkeys, you've had a full meal!

At the end of the day, the foreman called us together.

"Hey, if you're hungry, take some time and go upstairs and eat," he said.

Then he walked us into the freezer. There was a bare turkey

carcass sitting there. It was so naked I wanted to find it some clothes! Its breasts were sticking out and its legs had been picked to the bone! I guess I was a little hungrier than I thought!

Fortunately, the boss man didn't fire me. It was a good job, and I always had a little money in my pockets when I was a student.

When I arrived at Tommy's house the next day, Nancy wouldn't open the front door for me. She was looking through the peephole, and then she started ranting and raving at me. The woman went slap insane!

"What is your problem?" Nancy said.

She worked in the registrar's office at Louisiana Tech, so I figured she'd seen my grades. I knew I'd be on the next bus back to Gonzales, Louisiana, when Momma and Daddy found out I'd flunked out.

"Are you going to let me in?" I asked her.

She stood behind the door and hollered at me for the next five minutes.

"Hey, look, if you don't open the door, I'm going to go back to the dorm," I said.

She opened the door and screamed, "No, you're not. Get in here and sit down!" She pointed her finger at me and said, "Did you go check your grades?"

"No," I told her. "I couldn't care less what my grades are, because I'm not coming back."

She proceeded to chew my butt out for the next hour.

"You really didn't go look at your grades, did you?" she asked.

"No, I know I flunked out," I told her. "I don't care what my grades are. I know one thing—college is not for me."

By then, Tommy, Phil, and Harold were there, and they

started in on me as well. They were calling me stupid and lazy again.

"Hey, y'all might as well get off of that," Nancy told them.

"What do you mean?" Phil asked her.

"He partied for six months and never went to class and nearly made the dean's list," Nancy said. "He was three points from making an A average! He's obviously not too dumb!"

Hey, I told you C is always the correct answer.

"One time in Vietnam,
I saw a grizzly bear
riding a scooter."

Chapter

12

Big Oaf

EVEN THOUGH I EARNED my way onto the list of possible candidates for Louisiana Tech University's honors program, I didn't return to school for the next academic quarter in the spring of 1968. I knew going into my freshman year that college probably wasn't for me, but I gave it the old college try, and, hey, I proved to my older brothers that maybe they weren't smarter than me.

For whatever reason, I couldn't get into the routine of going to college. One of the things that really turned me off about higher education was that I met a lot of guys who had college degrees, and they told me they spent most of their time in classes like basket weaving and pottery. Then they'd tell me they majored in psychology! Hey, if you're going to become a psychologist, why are you learning how to make a basket and an ashtray? It doesn't make any sense to me. Some of the smartest people I know have sixth-grade educations and started working in the seventh grade because their families needed them to work. Conversely, some of the most educated idiots I've ever met have a master's degree or PhD. They couldn't pour urine out of a boot with the instructions written on the heel!

Breaking the news to Momma and Daddy wasn't easy. Even though I'd warned them about what was probably going to happen if they sent me to college, I knew they would be disappointed because each of my brothers and sisters was in school. They wanted me to have the same opportunity, and I'm sure they made some big sacrifices to make it happen. I think they might have even mortgaged the family farm to pay my tuition.

I broke the news to Daddy when we were driving to a duck hole one morning during Christmas break.

"Daddy, I ain't going back to school," I told him. "I know you and Momma really want me to go, but it ain't for me."

Daddy looked at me and sadly shook his head. I could see the disappointment in his eyes.

"Si, after all the sacrifices your mother and I made over the last few months to come up with the money to send you to college, you still say 'ain't,'" he said.

That was the end of our conversation.

After three quarters of college, I decided it was time for me to major in Si-cology. I was ready to get on living my life and finding my place in the world.

Of course, I knew Uncle Sam probably had other ideas for me. Phil, Tommy, and Nancy warned me that if I dropped out of college, I would probably get drafted into the military and be sent to Vietnam. American military advisers had been involved in the

Vietnam War since 1950, and then our involvement escalated in the early 1960s. The number of American troops in Vietnam tripled in 1961 and tripled again in 1962, and then U.S. combat troops were first deployed there in 1965 to fight the Vietcong and the spread of communism.

After Congress passed the Military Selective Service Act of 1967, if you were a male, at least eighteen years old, single, and not in college, you were going to Vietnam. Hey, I was four for four, Jack! Two weeks after I withdrew from Louisiana Tech, my draft papers arrived at my parents' house. I opened the letter and it basically said, "Uncle Sam wants you—right now!" A few weeks later, I reported to the army recruitment office in Shreveport, Louisiana, where they gave me a physical and determined I was fit to serve my country. Was there ever any doubt?

I went home to Dixie for about a month, and then I boarded a train in Shreveport in April 1968 for basic training at Fort Benning outside Columbus, Georgia. As soon as I stepped off the train, the drill sergeants were in my face screaming, "Get down, maggot!" My basic training lasted eight weeks, and it was miserable. It was the start of a hot, sticky Georgia summer. Hey, it was so hot and humid that I saw trees

Hey, it was so hot and humid that I saw trees fighting over dogs.

fighting over dogs. That's how thirsty they were! Even the squirrels were using suntan lotion! Growing up in Louisiana, I was used to the heat and humidity, but it's a lot more unbearable when you're going through basic training.

My basic training was especially hard because I had two drill sergeants with completely different personalities The first one lasted only a couple of weeks and left because of a death in his family. I didn't even know the man, but it wasn't very long until I was missing him more than my momma! After he left, a bunch of us were sitting on the barrack steps waiting for the next guy who was going to make our lives miserable. We saw a taxicab coming down the main road in the base, and there was something wrong with it. Most automobiles are equally balanced on four tires. But this taxi was leaning heavily to the right side! It looked like the right side of the taxi was going to grind the asphalt on the road!

When the taxi pulled up in front our barrack, King Kong climbed out of the backseat. My new drill sergeant was about six feet eight inches tall and weighed four hundred and fifty pounds! He was wearing a Smokey the Bear hat that I could have taken a bath in! The guy was enormous! He was a huge man! His name was Sergeant Oliver, but we called him the Big Oaf behind his back. It seemed that his objective was to make my life as painful as possible.

While the Big Oaf was determined to break me, I will give him credit for one thing. Fort Benning is an army Ranger base. Look, you do not walk on a Ranger base—you run everywhere! We ran to the mess hall, showers, latrines, barracks, and everywhere else we went. We ran while brushing our teeth! You did not walk; you did the airborne shuffle, which is running. As large as the Big Oaf was, he actually ran right next to us everywhere we went. You had to respect the man for that.

Big Oaf

One day in basic training, the Big Oaf woke us at five A.M. and informed us we were going on a ten-mile run. We ate breakfast and then loaded our packs onto our backs. About an hour later, after most of us had puked up our breakfast, the Big Oaf yelled, "Men, you're doing a great job. We've already covered five miles!"

I guess we felt like the end was in sight, because we picked up our pace. About an hour later, as we were really beginning to feel the weight of our packs, the Big Oaf yelled, "You're doing fine, men. Just fine! We should reach the starting point any minute now!"

As much as he tried, I was never really intimidated by the Big Oaf. Since I was from a large family and had so many older brothers, people getting in my face and yelling at me never really bothered me. But some guys couldn't handle it, and their lives were miserable during basic training. I always thought the hazing was funny, but my drill sergeants never found it to be very humorous. They didn't like that I was laughing or smiling the entire time. Somehow, I made it out of basic training alive.

On the day I graduated from basic training in June 1968, we were wearing our dress greens on the drill fields as we waited for the ceremony to start. The Big Oaf got in my face and was screaming at me again. It was almost as if he wanted one more shot at me. He started yelling, and, of course, I busted out laughing. I couldn't help it. It made him so mad. He yelled his favorite words: "Drop, maggot!"

I stood there and laughed at him.

"Hey, I'm in my dress greens," I told him. "I'm not getting down and getting dirty. You're out of your mind."

The Big Oaf looked at me in disbelief.

"Am I hearing you say what I think you said, Private Robertson?" he asked.

"Yeah, I ain't getting down and dirty," I told him.

"Am I going to have to put you in the front, leaning, rest position, maggot?" he asked.

"Are you serious?" I said.

"Dead serious," he yelled.

So I dropped and did twenty-five push-ups. I jumped up and was smiling again.

"Wrong answer, maggot!" the Big Oaf yelled.

I dropped down and gave him twenty-five more. I was in the greatest shape of my life, so it wasn't a problem, but I was obviously still as stubborn as a mule.

It took three hundred push-ups before the Big Oaf finally wiped the smile off of my face.

With my deployment to Vietnam right around the corner, I feared I wouldn't be smiling for much longer.

"Your beard is so dumb,
it takes two hours to watch *60 Minutes*! "

Chapter 13

Passing the Test

ONE OF THE MAIN reasons I left college and went into the military was because I didn't want to have to attend class—and I really didn't like taking tests. What's the first thing the army did with me once I graduated from basic training?

Uncle Sam gave me a test!

To assemble an effective fighting force, the United States Army believed it needed the right kind of man as well as the right kind of equipment in Vietnam. Hey, it didn't take the army long to realize it had the right kind of man on its hands, but it had to figure out what kind of equipment to put in my hands to make me a killing machine. When I joined the army, there were over three hundred occupations available. The army wanted to make sure it didn't waste my talents and abilities, so it gave me a long test to determine how I could help America the most.

Fortunately for me, it was a multiple-choice test!

Before the army assigned me to a unit, I was required to take the Army Classification Battery (ACB), which graded incoming soldiers in areas such as electronics repair, general maintenance, mechanical maintenance, clerical skills, radio code, surveillance and communications, and, of course, combat. If a soldier scored well in electronics repair, he would probably be assigned to something like missile or air defense repair. If a soldier scored well in general maintenance, he might be assigned to areas like construction and utilities. Someone who scored well in combat might end up in the infantry or armor units, and high marks in clerical skills usually correlated well to desk jobs.

Shortly after I was assigned to Advanced Infantry Training at Fort Lee in Virginia in the fall of 1968, I took the ACB for the first time. Hey, I can recite the alphabet after drinking a twelve-pack of soda pop while blindfolded and standing on one leg, so I knew the army's test wouldn't be a problem. A few days after I completed the test, my commanding officer called me into his office.

"Hey, Robertson, your smoke-blowing days are over," he told me.

"What are you talking about?" I asked him.

"The ole country-boy act you've got going isn't going to cut it anymore," he said. "You're in the top five percent in the world."

"What world are you talking about?" I asked.

"What don't you understand?" he said. "You just scored higher than ninety-five percent of the army on the ACB. You're on the fast track."

Now, you have to understand one thing: people were bombing the ACB worldwide in the army in 1968. It was a big scandal throughout the military, and the Pentagon couldn't figure out if the test was flawed or if its troops really weren't that smart! A seventy was considered a passing score on the ACB. I scored a sixty-nine! Somehow, I was still better than nearly everybody else entering the army at the time.

When I saw my test results, I was surprised to see the areas in which I scored the highest. I scored extremely high in architecture and engineering, followed by clerical, mechanical maintenance, and surveillance and communications. As I sat there looking at my scores, I pondered what my vocation was going to be in the military. Would I be a spy? Hey, I'm kind of like Victoria. She has her secrets and so do I! Need a secret Santa? I'm your man! The Vietcong would never detect me behind enemy lines. I'm the master of distractions! A couple of hand gestures and—*bam!*—I'll pull the underwear clean off your butt!

Hey, I'm kind of like Victoria. She has her secrets and so do I!

While espionage sounded enticing, so did the possibility of being a mechanic or engineer. My brothers and I were always building and fixing things when we were growing up. If our bicycles or boat motors broke, we had to fix them because we sure weren't getting new ones. We built forts, bridges, duck blinds, and dams when we were young. How much different could Vietnam really be from Louisiana?

I even thought about going into the military police or becoming a cook. Hey, I'd rather eat my cooking than what I ate in Vietnam. I am the MacGyver of cooking. If you bring me a piece of bread, cabbage, coconut, mustard greens, pig's feet, pinecones, and a woodpecker, I'll make a great chicken pot pie. One time I cooked a big pot of soup. The label on the packaging said to empty the entire contents into the broth. Well, Miss Kay got a twenty-cent coupon in her bowl of soup. At least she saved some money on her next trip to the grocery store!

There were so many career choices in the army, and it was difficult to pick only one.

At first, the army sent me to sniper school after I graduated from Advanced Infantry Training. I guess they figured if I could shoot squirrels and ducks, I could hold my own on the battlefield and shoot Charlie. But I was only in sniper school for about a week. After a few days, I asked one of the instructors, "Hey, when are we going to shoot?" He told me we had three more weeks of classes before we would get our rifles. Well, you know how I am about attending classes.

"Uh-uh," I told him. "Send me to a unit."

Now, just because the army gives you a test doesn't necessarily mean it's going to put you in a job that best utilizes your skills. The army tried to put people in areas where they could help it the most, but they weren't always good at doing it. If the army had a truck driver and a computer engineer, you would think the former would drive a truck and the latter would work with computers. Uh-uh, not in the army. No, let's switch it. The truck driver worked on computers and the computer engineer drove the truck. The army liked to break a man down and mold him into what it wanted. It didn't make any sense, but that's how they did it.

Passing the Test

I was assigned to be a readiness noncommissioned officer (NCO) in the areas of materials supply and accounting. My job was supervising supply requests, receipt, and storage, and maintaining an account of individual and organizational equipment. I was like the equipment manager of the army. If a soldier wanted something in Vietnam, he had to come see me. Need a new pair of socks? I'm the man to see. Need ammunition for your M16? I'm the guy. Most days, it was a pretty smooth process when soldiers came to see me. But if I was having a bad day, hey, all bets were off. Grab a Snickers bar, because you're not going anywhere for a while, Jack!

I was also involved in the day-to-day operations of transporting soldiers, mobilization planning, maintenance, pay, and guard duty. I was basically the commander's right-hand man. I did whatever he told me to do. Now, I did not wear hard stripes. There were hard-striped soldiers in Vietnam and there were specialists. A hard-striped soldier specialized in combat and war; a specialist was someone like the military police or a medic. We were specialists in something other than actual fighting. Everybody in the army was trained to fight, but some of us were put in areas of support off the battlefield.

After I graduated from Advanced Infantry Training, they sent the notice of deployments to our barrack. Obviously, everyone was hoping to avoid Vietnam, but I always knew that was where I was going to be deployed. I didn't know why, but I knew in the bottom of my heart that's where I was going. Well, guys with last names that started with A to R were sent to Germany. Somehow the list of last names beginning with R ended before Robertson. Then I and every guy with a last name after mine were sent to Vietnam. I was the only soldier from my company who was immediately deployed to Vietnam. Later, I found out the guys who went to Germany were only there for a couple of weeks of training and then were sent to Vietnam.

A couple of weeks before I was scheduled to leave for Vietnam, a few of my buddies and I went to see a movie during a weekend pass. John Wayne had just finished making a war movie about Vietnam. It was called *The Green Berets*. It was about an army colonel who picked two teams of Green Berets to complete a dangerous mission in South Vietnam. We went to see the movie at a theater, and it scared every one of us. Even though the movie was fictional, the images looked real to me. It was the first time I'd seen war. I knew Vietnam was where I was fixing to go, and it didn't look like a very nice place. In fact, it scared me to death.

"Hey, I gotta work
with what I've got.
It's called improv-isavation."

Chapter 14

Good Morning, Vietnam!

MY FEET HIT THE ground in South Vietnam on October 19, 1968. Several guys told me their stories about flying into Vietnam, and a lot of them were pretty wild and scary. They told me about being bombarded with rockets and missiles as their jets landed. My arrival was pretty uneventful. We flew into the Can Tho airfield and climbed off the plane. It was eerily quiet until somebody said, "Welcome to Nam."

Perhaps the thing I remember most about arriving in Vietnam is being overwhelmed by the smell of fish. Now, I grew up on the river, and my brothers and I were always fishing or cleaning fish, but this was different. I smelled fish everywhere I went. The South Vietnamese ate a lot of fish, and commercial fishing was one of their major sources of income. It wasn't necessarily a bad smell, but it was the only thing you could smell! Hey, how do you stop a fish from smelling? You cut off its nose, Jack! I was ready to cut my nose off after only a couple of weeks in Vietnam. When I returned home after my twelve-month enlistment, I couldn't stand the smell of fish. I couldn't even stomach the smell when I went to Phil's house on the Ouachita River years later. It's one of the reasons Phil gave up fishing altogether after he quit working as a commercial fisherman. Phil was around fish so much as a commercial fisherman that he didn't want to be near them after he quit. I'm the same way when it comes to fish, even more than forty years after I left Vietnam.

Can Tho is the largest city in the Mekong Delta and is about seventy-five miles southwest of Ho Chi Minh City (which was called Saigon when I was in Vietnam). It sits near the Mekong River and is the delta's commercial hub. Today, Can Tho produces about half the country's rice. Rice paddies, low-lying marshes, and mangrove swamps surround the city, as does a vast system of natural and man-made canals. There were floating markets where you could buy fish, fruits, and vegetables. I'm sure it's a beautiful city now, but it wasn't very picturesque when I was there, at least not to me.

While I was deployed to Vietnam, I lived in a three-story hotel in downtown Can Tho. The army base in Can Tho wasn't big enough to have barracks to house all of the troops, so a bunch of soldiers stayed in hotels with names like the Pink Palace, Cheap Charlie's, and the Mekong Hotel. From what I remember, the hotel I stayed in was far from a palace, and I'm sure the rent was pretty cheap for Uncle Sam.

Fortunately for me, I arrived in Can Tho about nine months after the Tet Offensive. On January 31, 1968, the Vietcong and North Vietnamese launched a series of surprise attacks against

South Vietnam, American forces, and our allies during what was supposed to be a two-day cease-fire during the Tet lunar new year celebration. More than seventy thousand North Vietnamese and Vietcong troops attacked more than one hundred cities and towns in South Vietnam, including the Can Tho airfield, which is where I primarily worked.

It took American forces about three days to clear Can Tho of Vietcong troops. Although U.S. and South Vietnamese forces fought back most of the attacks, the Tet Offensive was a major turning point in the Vietnam War. The North Vietnamese and Vietcong put the U.S. on notice that they were more organized and stronger than we suspected.

In a civil war like was happening in Vietnam, it's hard to figure out who's fighting for what side. What most people don't understand about the military is that if you go to a foreign country, sometimes they don't speak your language and don't want you there. In other words, most of the people there don't like you. Hey, I wasn't trying to make friends in Vietnam. My only goal was to complete my twelve months and get back to Louisiana as quickly as possible.

Although I was there for only one year, it was a really difficult time in my life. It was the first time I'd been away from my parents, brothers, and sisters, and I was thousands of miles across the Pacific Ocean from home. I wasn't quite sure why we were fighting in a land so far from home, but I was bound and determined not to get myself killed while I was there.

One of the things I remember most about being in Vietnam is watching movies on the roof of the hotel where I was living. We had a movie projector set up and we sat and watched movies nearly every night. When I first got to Vietnam, I sat on the roof and watched guys going out. They'd leave sober, but then they'd come staggering back drunk a few hours later. I always thought, *That's not going to be me.* But a few months later, guys sat on the same roof and watched me come back stumbling drunk.

Believe me, it was easy to find a drink in Can Tho if you wanted one. Of course, you had to be careful where you went because the Vietcong also used Can Tho as an R & R spot. Charlie would dress like a Vietnamese peasant and walk right into town for some rest and relaxation. Most of the watering holes were filled with bar girls, some of whom made so much money from American troops that they bought estates in the countryside! You could find a drink and a girl whenever you wanted for the right price.

It was the only time in my life when I drank heavily. Now, I partied during my short stay at Louisiana Tech, but it was different in Vietnam. I was largely drinking to forget where I was. When you're in a place like Vietnam, you get to a point where you don't care anymore. You're in a place that's foreign to you, and you know for a fact that many people there hate you and will kill you if they get the chance. It really does something to your mind to know that many of the people living around you don't like you and want you to die.

It was the only time in my life when I drank heavily.

Believe it or not, I came close to killing two people in Vietnam. Shortly after I arrived there, I was on guard duty in a tower at the airfield. I had an M14 rifle and a slingshot. Guess what Vietnamese children liked to do for fun? They liked to throw rocks at the American guards in the watchtowers. I kept a handful of rocks in one of my ammunition pouches just in case I became a target. One day while I was on guard duty, a rock nailed me on the side of my head. I touched my hair and my hand was covered in blood. I thought I'd been shot! I looked down and saw a Vietnamese boy laughing and pointing at me. I clicked my gun and started to aim to shoot him. Thankfully, I came to my senses and didn't do it. The next time I was hit by a rock, I returned fire with my slingshot. Before too long, I was having regular slingshot wars with the Vietnamese children around our airfield. It didn't take them long to figure out that I was a better shot than them!

The other time I nearly took a life, I was waiting for a truck to pick me up and felt a tap on my kidney. I turned around and saw a huge snake staring right at me. A Vietnamese woman—we called them momma-sans—had a boa constrictor wrapped around her neck. It was big enough to eat her if it wanted. "You want to buy the snake?" she asked me. I grabbed my gun and was fixing to shoot her and the snake! I'm not sure if I could have ever shot Charlie if I had to, but I was ready to shoot her!

Here's how bad it got for me during my twelve months in Vietnam: A buddy and me came up with the brilliant idea of us volunteering to be door gunners in helicopters. At the time, the life expectancy of a door gunner in Vietnam was about three days. When one was killed, the army put another soldier in his place. It was about the most dangerous job in the war, and my buddy and I were getting ready to volunteer for it! Fortunately, I came to my senses before we signed up. I must have been insane to even be thinking about it!

I drank so much beer and whiskey in Vietnam that I decided I would quit drinking alcohol altogether once I returned home. I saw what alcohol was doing to me in Vietnam and realized I needed to stop for good.

But I had to make it home alive for that to happen.

"I don't like uniforms.
Hey, right now
I want to kick my own butt!"

Chapter 15

Deuce and a Half

S HORTLY AFTER I ARRIVED in Vietnam, some of the soldiers who had been there for a while gave me a few tips on how to survive. One of the most important things they told me was to make sure all of my personal belongings were locked down at all times because the Vietnamese loved to steal from Americans. Now, Momma and Daddy had taught me that stealing was a sin—"Thou shalt not steal" is one of the Ten Commandments—so I found it hard to believe that the nice Vietnamese people would steal from the very people who were sent there to protect them.

"What are you talking about?" I asked one of the soldiers.

"These people will steal anything and everything," he said.

"Hey, I don't believe you," I said. "Give me an example."

"These people will steal your radio and leave the music," he said.

"Now, that's a thief!" I told him.

It didn't take me long to figure out he was telling the truth. One of my daily duties in Vietnam was to drive troops from our hotel to the Can Tho airfield in the morning and then back to the hotel at the end of the workday. I transported the troops in a two-and-a-half-ton cargo truck—we called it a deuce and a half—and it didn't have a canvas over the bed or rails on its sides. The army started using the M35 family of trucks in 1949 and utilized them all the way through Operation Iraqi Freedom. Obviously, they were good, dependable trucks. The truck had a ten-tire configuration, so it could carry as much as twenty thousand pounds of cargo on the road. It was a very versatile truck in a war zone.

One day, before I made the drive back to the hotel, which was only about one mile, I walked around my truck and gave it a thorough inspection. I was required to inspect the truck every time I climbed behind the steering wheel to make sure it was working properly and hadn't been booby-trapped by the Vietcong. I saw that each of the ten tires was there and was inflated properly and didn't notice anything else suspicious. After I gave a thumbs-up, the troops loaded up in the bed of the truck, and I pulled out to drive back to the hotel. But on this particular day, for whatever reason, there was a lot of traffic in downtown Can Tho, so the drive took a little longer than usual. Even though the traffic was crazy, I never had to completely stop and probably didn't drive less than ten miles per hour.

I arrived at the hotel and the troops started to unload. I locked up the steering wheel, locked the doors, and then started to walk to the hotel.

"Hey, Robertson," one of the soldiers yelled to me. "You're missing a tire."

"Yeah, sure," I said.

"No, seriously, you're missing a tire off the back," he said.

"Good grief," I said, knowing the soldier was probably trying to play a trick on me.

I walked back to the truck and saw a lug nut sticking out of where one of the dual back tires used to be. Someone stole a tire while I was driving back to the hotel!

"Y'all didn't see anything?" I asked a few of the soldiers, who had gathered around the truck.

"Nah," one of them said. "We didn't see anything."

"Hey, look, all of the tires were on this truck when we left the airfield," I said. "I never stopped. Y'all were sitting in the back. You didn't see anything?"

"Nope," one of them said.

"Something's not right with this picture," I said. "You're sitting above the tires, you idiots. You had to have seen or heard something!"

"Nah, we didn't hear or see anything," one of them said.

I sat there looking at the lug nut while scratching my head and trying to figure out what had just happened.

"The lug nuts must have been loose," one of them said. "The tire must have fallen off."

We didn't have loose lug nuts on a deuce and a half. When we put tires and lug nuts on a deuce and a half, we had to stand on the tire iron to make sure they were tight. There wasn't any way the lug nuts were loose.

The only plausible explanation was that a Vietnamese person

stole a tire while I was driving down the road! NASCAR pit crews don't work that fast, Jack! I know it might be hard to believe, but it's exactly what happened!

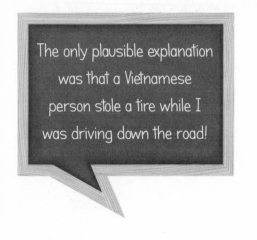

Now, I've never had much patience for thieves. A thief is someone who is too lazy to work for what he wants, so he'll steal from someone else. I've read about smart thieves and not-so-smart thieves. In the Czech Republic last year, a band of thieves stole a ten-ton bridge! They arrived at a depot and informed the workers they'd been hired to disassemble the bridge to make way for a new one. The thieves walked away with millions of dollars in scrap metal before anyone figured out the bridge wasn't supposed to come down! Now, that's a thief, Jack!

Last year, a man snatched a woman's purse while she walked through a park in Georgia. When police located a man matching the suspect's description, they put him into a police cruiser and returned to the scene of the crime. Police told him to exit the vehicle and face the victim for an ID. He looked and her and said, "Yeah, that's the woman I robbed." Hey, at least he was honest!

The Lord tells us we're supposed to love everyone, so I don't hate thieves. I guess there's even a place in heaven for them. At least I can respect their ingenuity, and they're still more likable than most of the attorneys I've met.

One day, a teacher, a petty thief, and a lawyer died and went to heaven. St. Peter met them at the gates and said, "Sorry, heaven's about filled up, so you'll have to answer a question correctly to come in."

St. Peter looked at the teacher and asked, "What's the name of the famous ocean liner that sank in the Atlantic Ocean after hitting an iceberg?"

"The *Titanic,*" she said.

"Correct," St. Peter said. "Come on in."

Then St. Peter turned to the thief.

"How many people died on the ship?" he asked.

"Ooooh, that's a difficult question," the thief said. "But I saw the movie, and I think the answer is about one thousand and five hundred."

"Close enough," St. Peter said. "Come on in."

Finally, St. Peter turned to the lawyer.

"Name each of the deceased," he said.

Hey, let me tell you how bad the Vietnamese were about stealing. One of the army's platoons had set up shop on a mountainside above a village in the Mekong Delta. They were on a reconnaissance mission, going from village to village to determine whether Charlie had infiltrated them or not. For whatever reason, they kept burning up power generators and losing electricity at their base camp. They couldn't figure out what was happening. No matter what they did, they were burning up brand-new generators every night! The motor officer was yanking his hair out trying to figure it out. Every night before they turned them on, they checked the oil and made sure they were operating correctly, but they kept burning up in the middle of the night.

Finally, one of the officers decided he was going to get to the bottom of it. The generators usually ran on two hundred and twenty volts, but you could convert them to four hundred and forty volts. One night, the officer shut down the generators and switched them to four hundred and forty volts. After he turned the generators back on, the village became extremely bright. It looked like the Las Vegas Strip! All of the sudden, it sounded like fireworks. TVs, radios, and all the other appliances in the village were blowing up! It looked like a firefight in the bush.

The officer sent a few soldiers down the hillside and they discovered a string of extension cords that probably covered two miles from the generators to the village! Every night, one of the Vietnamese villagers snuck up the hill and plugged the cord into the generators. The Vietnamese watched TV all night on Uncle Sam!

Now, that's a thief, Jack!

"I'm like Aretha Franklin.
Don't get any R-E-S-P-E-C-T
round this joint!"

Chapter
16

Guard Duty

ONE OF MY FIRST jobs in Vietnam was working in a warehouse in the back of Can Tho Airfield. Every chance I had, I rode in a rough-terrain forklift with the guy who was operating it. I rode with him for about six months to learn how to drive it. I figured if something happened to the guy who was driving it, I'd be next in line to jump into the driver's seat. Driving the forklift would keep me out of harm's way if nothing else. Hey, I might have been born at night, but it wasn't last night, Jack!

Mostly, we loaded and unloaded supplies from cargo planes and moved crates to where they needed to be. But every now and then, we'd get in a Jeep, deuce and a half, or five-ton cargo truck that had been shot up by the Vietcong. Our job was to go over the vehicle and strip it down, taking every working part we could possibly use. We'd set aside the tires, wheels, motors, batteries, transmissions, carburetors, water pumps, and any other parts we could salvage. Normally, only the metal frame of the Jeep or cargo truck was left. We'd pick up the truck or Jeep frame with the forklift and drop it into a pond at the back of the airfield.

Hey, I might have been born at night, but it wasn't last night, Jack!

Well, as I suspected, the guy who was driving the forklift left Vietnam when his enlistment in the army was over. A sergeant came up to me and said, "Hey, we need somebody to drive the forklift. Do you know how to do it?"

"Hey, can you crank it?" I asked.

"I've been watching you ride around with him for six months," the sergeant said. "You never saw him crank it?"

"Nah, I never saw him do it," I said. "Do you want me to do everything around here?"

So the sergeant climbed into the forklift and cranked it up.

"Get out of the way," I told him.

From that day forward, my job was to drive the rough-terrain forklift in the warehouse and motor pool at the airfield. Some nights, I also had to take my turn on guard duty at the airfield. I usually guarded the motor pool, where they kept the Jeeps, trucks, and other vehicles we used in the army. The motor pool extended all the way to the edge of the pond where we dumped the stripped truck and Jeep frames.

Guard Duty

One day, we had a brand-new deuce-and-a-half diesel engine come to us in a metal box. New engines were like gold in Vietnam. Most of our vehicles were pretty outdated, so it was rare that we acquired new equipment. The technicians in the motor pool took the engine out of the box, hooked a battery to it, and cranked it to make sure it was running properly. Then they bolted it back down because they planned to put it in a deuce and a half the next morning.

That night, a buddy and I were on guard duty. We had to cover a pretty big compound, so we started the night walking the fence in opposite directions. About an hour later, we hooked back up again for a cigarette break.

"You see anything?" I asked him.

"Nah, I didn't see anything," he said.

"Nah, me neither," I said.

Suddenly, we heard some noise coming from the motor pool area. I called the watchtower and told them to pop a flare over the motor pool. They fired a flare and it lit up the entire area. We scanned the motor pool and didn't see anything. We checked under and inside every vehicle to make sure Charlie wasn't hiding anywhere. We didn't find anything suspicious.

I called the watchtower again and told them to shoot a flare over the pond. I wanted to make sure our suspects weren't swimming back across the pond, which separated the American army compound from the South Vietnamese military base.

When a flare lit up the sky again, I looked out at the pond and saw the brand-new deuce-and-a-half engine floating on the water. There was a Vietnamese person swimming on each side of it. The two men were swimming with one arm while holding the engine with the other. They were stroking their free arms kind of like the Olympians do in the butterfly stroke.

Now, you have to understand that this was a 478-cubic-inch engine that probably weighed close to 1,650 pounds. I looked closer to see if the engine was floating on a raft but didn't see one. I looked to see if the Vietnamese had magically built a bridge across the pond but didn't see one.

As my buddy and I watched the Vietnamese in amazement, they stroked the engine all the way across the pond. The pond was more than one hundred yards wide!

I'll never forget the expression on my buddy's face after the Vietnamese reached the other side of the pond. Neither one of us said anything, but he had the dumbest look on his face. Then he smiled.

After I picked my jaw up off the ground, I asked him, "What did you see?"

"You first," he said.

"Let me start this conversation out this way," I said. "Did you see any kind of flotation device around that diesel engine?"

"Nah," he said.

"Are you sure you didn't see any kind of flotation device?" I asked him again.

"Uh-uh," he said.

"Well, how many people did you see?" I asked.

"One on each side," he said.

"Did you see any kind of raft?" I asked him.

"Nope," he said.

"Did you see any kind of bridge?" I asked.

"Nope," he said.

"Well, how are we going to report this in the morning?" I asked him.

"I'd rather not report it," he said.

"Hey, they're going to be missing that diesel engine in the morning, and then they're going to come looking for us," I said. "They're going to ask us why we weren't doing our jobs while we were on guard duty. We're going to have to report it. A brand-new diesel engine just doesn't get up and walk away."

"I don't know what we're going to say," he said.

"All I know is we can tell the truth," I said. "Did you see one Vietnamese on both sides of the engine?"

"Yep, that's what I saw," he said.

"Well, that's what we're telling them," I said.

"Sounds good to me," he said.

I knew no one was going to believe us.

When I gave my report to the officer in charge the next morning, he said, "Hey, y'all were smoking weed, weren't you?"

"I don't smoke weed, sir," I told him.

"Well, then you were drunk," he said.

"Hey, on a bad day, you might have me on the alcohol use because I keep a fifth of liquor in my pocket," I said. "But I don't drink while I'm on guard duty."

Well, after my buddy and I were interrogated for the next few hours, they finally believed our story, or at least they couldn't come up with another plausible explanation as to what happened to the engine.

My commanding officer sent two MPs in a Jeep to the other side of the pond. Much to their amazement, they found the deuce-and-a-half engine inside the South Vietnamese military compound and brought it back to the American side.

All these years later, I'm still not exactly sure how deep the water was in the pond. Day after day for six months, I watched Jeep and truck frames get dropped into the pond, so it was obviously pretty deep water.

What I do know is the pond was deep enough for fifty Vietnamese soldiers to stand on each other's shoulders and carry a diesel engine for more than one hundred yards.

And, boy, the Vietnamese sure can hold their breath.

"A beaver is like a ninja—
the suckers only work at night
and they're hard to find."

Chapter 17

Leave It to Beavers

HEY, MY HAT IS off to the Vietnamese. They're some of the most resourceful people I've ever seen. In a lot of ways, they were like beavers: they worked only at night, they were relentless, and they didn't stop working until the job was finished. Hey, it's hard to capture or kill something if it only moves at night. Beavers are hard to kill and so were the Vietnamese. It's the reason the Vietnam War lasted so long; the North Vietnamese and Vietcong continued to fight us even though they were grossly outmanned. They didn't think they could lose, and they took advantage of their natural surroundings.

Look, you know what's un-be-beaver-able? In 2010, scientists discovered that beavers had constructed a dam of trees, branches, grasses, and mud in Alberta, Canada, that was more than half a mile long! The dam is located in a remote part of Wood Buffalo

National Park, and park rangers didn't even know it was there until scientists saw it on satellite images from outer space! Scientists say the dam is the largest in the world and that the beavers have probably been building it since the 1970s.

Hey, you know how I feel about beavers. I believe they're the pelted plague. The furry rodents are nothing more than log-chewing, water-slapping, flat-tailed rascals! Phil and I always have problems with them on our hunting land. They're our bucktoothed archnemeses. Beavers like to dam up water, which prevents it from reaching the land around our duck blinds. Look, it's pretty simple: if there's no water, there's no ducks. So there are few things that are more enjoyable to me than blowing up a beaver dam. It's like I tell Phil: hey, give them a kiss for me—the kiss of death!

I didn't know why beavers have flat tails until I went to Vietnam. Shortly after I arrived there, one of the American soldiers warned me to never go into the jungle at night. Now, I wouldn't have been caught dead in the jungle even during daylight, but I was curious to know why I shouldn't go in there at night.

"Because elephants jump out of the trees at night," he said.

Hey, now you know why beavers have flat tails. They go into the jungle at night, Jack!

While I despise beavers, I also respect their work ethic and determination. Do you know how hard it is to build dams and lodges? A lodge is a hollow mound of sticks, stones, and mud, and beavers live and sleep inside of them. Beavers usually build them on the banks or islands of a stream or river. The entrance to the lodge is underwater, so beavers first build a dam across the river to prevent the entrance from freezing during the winter. Hey, when two beavers walk into the house, the first one always tells the other one, "Hey, shut the dam door!"

Leave It to Beavers

Beavers work together to build their dams and lodges, kind of like we do when we're building duck calls. It's a collective effort. With their long, sharp teeth, beavers chew through thick trees. Hey, beavers are even smart enough to make sure the trees always fall toward their dams! They drag tree limbs with their teeth and push logs to the dam with their noses. Beavers even roll large stones on the logs to keep them in place. Hey, you want to talk about some busy beavers!

When the beavers are finished constructing a lodge, they cover the walls with mud to insulate them and keep out predators, whether it's foxes, wolverines, snakes, bears, Grizzly Adams, coyotes, or Daniel Boone. If a predator manages to break its way into the lodge, the beavers are able to escape through a secret exit. See, when beavers first start building a lodge, they burrow a secret tunnel on the other side of the river, which leads back to their lodge underwater. Now, tell me beavers aren't smart!

When I was in Vietnam, it was like we were fighting some really mean beavers. They were ferocious, Jack! One of the first things American troops did when they built a new camp in the Mekong Delta was bring in engineers and bulldozers to clear about two hundred yards of bush for a firing zone. If the Vietcong attacked them, they wanted a clear area to fire mortars, grenades, or whatever else they wanted to repel them. As soon as the firing zone was cleared, the Americans built bunkers around the perimeter, giving our troops shelter and protection in case we were attacked. Well, at one forward base, the American troops dug bunkers around the perimeter just before dark. When they awoke the next morning, they discovered the Vietnamese had dug a bunker in front of every bunker they'd made! Their bunkers were even finished with roofs, hot tubs, and satellite dishes! Our bunkers were only holes in the ground. I

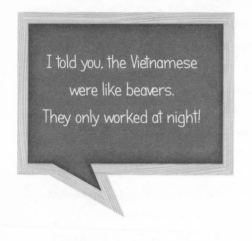

I told you, the Vietnamese were like beavers. They only worked at night!

told you, the Vietnamese were like beavers. They only worked at night!

And, hey, you want to talk about smart! One of the American military's main objectives during the Vietnam War was to blow up bridges along the Ho Chi Minh Trail to cut off the Vietcong's supply lines. The Ho Chi Minh Trail ran from North Vietnam to South Vietnam, snaking through neighboring Laos and Cambodia along the way. Our air force flew over the trail and bombed bridges, wiping nearly every one of them out. After a few months, the Americans realized the Vietcong were still moving supplies along the Ho Chi Minh Trail. They were still getting materials to South Vietnam, even without the bridges.

Well, a few high-ranking officers assembled a couple of Special Forces teams for a reconnaissance mission to find out how the Vietcong were doing it. After a few weeks of hiding in the bush, the Americans saw a trail of truck lights coming. The trucks were barely visible coming down a mountain. When the trucks pulled up to a river, they just kept coming, even though the bridge had been wiped out! The trucks drove through the water and came out on the other side. Hey, the Vietcong built a bridge about three feet underwater. The U.S. Air Force couldn't even see the underwater bridges to blow them up.

And you want to talk about bold! One time, the Vietcong dug a tunnel under an American headquarters in Vietnam and listened to our high-ranking officers giving commands. The Americans were preparing to sweep an area where there were more than 100,000 Vietcong troops. But when American troops swept the area, there wasn't a soul in sight. Hey, the Vietcong listened to our orders and got everybody out. When the Americans left, the Vietcong moved back in. When I left South Vietnam in October 1969, there were two battalions of North Vietnamese army troops working the area around Can Tho. A gunship finally located one battalion moving across an opening, but there was still a second battalion on the loose. And we could never find them!

Sometimes the North Vietnamese were right under our noses and we didn't even know it! In the Seven Mountains region of the Mekong Delta, American troops kept bombing a mountain to drive out Vietcong forces. But every time the Americans sent in a recon patrol, they took heavy fire and had to retreat. So the Americans sent in more B-52 bombers, artillery fire, and rockets. They hammered the mountain day after day for a couple of weeks, but American troops kept taking fire when they tried to capture the mountain. After bombing it every day for three months, the Americans finally took the mountain. When American troops went inside a cave in the mountain, they found a ten-story hospital inside! There were operating rooms, recovery rooms, and offices for the North Vietnamese and Vietcong troops that came through the area. There was an American airfield right around the corner from the mountain, but we never even knew the hospital was there! Good night!

Hey, at least beavers slap the water with their tails to let us know they're there.

"I don't know any redneck who's not into fun. That's their middle name: Red Fun Neck!"

Chapter 18

Black Market

WHILE I WAS IN Vietnam, I became sort of a psychologist for several of the soldiers from Bravo Company, who were the infantry and foot soldiers. They were some of the bravest soldiers in Vietnam and always seemed to be in the line of fire. Well, the army liked to give the guys who'd been beating the bush for eleven months a couple of weeks to cool off before they shipped them back to the United States. I guess Uncle Sam figured there wasn't any better place to do it than my hotel room. There was always an empty bunk in my hotel room in Can Tho, and a lot of the guys from Eleventh Bravo ended up staying in my room for a couple of weeks.

Hey, while they were cleansing their minds and relaxing, they liked to tell a lot of their stories to me. My empty bunk became Dr. Phil's sofa! I listened to their stories with an inquir-

ing mind, and a lot of guys liked to bounce their fears and problems off of me.

You wouldn't believe some of the stories I heard! One guy
showed up and stayed in my hotel room for three weeks. We became pretty good friends, and he told me about how the Vietcong
attacked their camp one night. He said three of their guys were
badly hurt during the attack, and the medic immediately started
treating their wounds. The medic attended to one guy, leaned him
up against a tree, and then started patching up the next guy.

Well, after the medic patched up the second guy's shoulder, he
moved on to the third guy, who was shot in the leg. All of a sudden, they heard the second guy screaming. A tiger had attacked
him and was dragging him back into the jungle! The medic and
the other two guys started shooting at the tiger and scared it back
into the bush. It was one of the most frightening stories I heard in
Vietnam.

Fortunately for me, I avoided most of the dangerous missions
in Vietnam. But one day, my colonel came to me and closed my
hotel room door.

"This conversation never took place," he said.

Uh-oh, I thought to myself. *I'm in trouble now.*

The colonel reached into his pocket and handed me three
thousand piastres, which was Vietnamese money.

"Go get me a Jeep engine," he said.

"Say what?" I asked. "Why did you come to me? What do you
expect me to do?"

"You have the money," he said. "Go find me a Jeep engine."

Hey, I didn't know what to do. I went and found one of the
guys staying in my room. He'd been in Vietnam for more than
three years and was always downtown. He spoke good Vietnam-

ese, so I figured he knew a bunch of the locals and where to find a Jeep engine.

"Hey, Kelly," I said. "Look, I need to go get a Jeep engine. Can you help me?"

"Sure, I know where to go," Kelly said. "No problem. When do you need it?"

"Now," I said.

"What are we going to drive?" Kelly asked.

"Hey, I guess we'll take the deuce and a half," I said. "We're going to need somewhere to put the engine."

"Meet me in the lobby in an hour," Kelly said.

An hour later, I met Kelly in the lobby and we loaded up in the deuce and a half. We drove downtown, and he told me to pull the truck into a narrow alley.

"Hey, this truck won't fit into the alley," I said.

"Sure it will," he said. "Pull the truck all the way to the end."

Sure enough, the truck fit into the alley with only a couple of feet to spare on each side. When we reached the end, Kelly jumped out and disappeared for a few minutes. He came back with a short Vietnamese man.

"Get out," Kelly told me.

I jumped out of the truck. The Vietnamese man proceeded to blindfold Kelly and me.

"Where are we going?" I asked.

"You don't need to know," the Vietnamese man said.

Over the next several minutes, we walked through a maze of alleys and doorways, and then they loaded us into a car. We drove around Can Tho for about thirty minutes. I knew I was going to die when we stopped!

When we finally stopped, I heard a door open. We walked

into a building, and then someone took our blindfolds off. When I opened my eyes, the only thing I could see was hundreds of large green containers. "Property of the U.S. Army" was stamped on the side of every container! There were engines for Jeeps, helicopters, and trucks lined up against the wall for nearly three hundred yards. It was like an auto parts store. They had whatever the army needed because they'd stolen it from us.

"We need a Jeep engine," Kelly said. "Give them the money, Robertson."

"Hey, this ain't the deal," I said. "I want to see the Jeep engine on our truck. You sure are a trusting soul. We don't even know where we are."

"Just give them the money," he said. "The engine will be on the back of the truck when we get back. I've done this before."

Against my better judgment, I handed the Vietnamese man the money, knowing I'd never see it or him again. And I knew there wouldn't be an engine on our truck, either.

Well, they blindfolded us again and drove us back to our truck. When I opened my eyes, I couldn't believe it when I saw a Jeep engine in the back of it.

The Vietnamese man shook my hand and said, "Nice doing business with you!"

Hey, now I buy everything through the black market: designer jeans, boots, high-definition TVs, toasters, kidneys, livers, and Swatch watches. It's the only way to do business!

I'll never forget the time a Bravo Company soldier stayed in my room for a couple of weeks shortly before I was sent home. The only things the guy carried with him were an M16 rifle, ammunition, and a small rucksack that had pineapple grenades hanging from it. I was beginning to wonder how crazy the guy actually was. One night, the guys staying next to us—our rooms were only separated by thin partitions—got drunk and started getting rowdy. They were throwing beer cans and boots at us. The guy staying with me started to get really upset. He'd been chasing Charlie for nearly a year, while trying to stay alive, and the last thing he wanted to deal with was a few drunks! Well, when a boot hit the mosquito net over the guy's bed, he nearly lost it. He went next door and told them to settle down.

A few seconds later, the guys threw another boot at him.

The guy staying with me reached under his bed, grabbed a pineapple grenade, and popped the pin. Then he threw it over the partition into the next room! Hey, I was lying against the wall to the other room. I grabbed my thin mattress and wrapped my body in it. I was expecting the grenade to explode and blow me into the next room! When the grenade landed in the next room, it sounded like something out of a cartoon. The three guys over there started scurrying for cover. I thought they were all going to die!

> The guy staying with me reached under his bed, grabbed a pineapple grenade, and popped the pin.

Well, the guy in my room was standing in our door, laughing his butt off. I thought he was slap insane! He walked into the next room, grabbed the grenade, came back, and threw it at me.

"Hey, it's a dud!" he said. "They reacted the same way Charlie does when I throw one into their bunker. There's one big difference, though. The Vietcong doesn't get to run. When I throw it into their bunker, I mow them down as they scurry out!"

I looked at him and said, "Man, you're about half a bubble off. You're not right."

I'm telling you: Vietnam did something to your mind if you were over there too long. Another guy who stayed in my room had been in Vietnam since the war started. He was on his sixth tour of duty. He was going home for leave and coming back for a seventh tour!

"Hey, man," I told him. "You've done your part for your country. You've done your share and five other guys' shares. You have a wife and two beautiful daughters. Go home and stay there! Good grief."

"Hey, I'm going home for thirty days to enjoy my family," he said. "Then I'm coming back here and kill some more Vietcong."

"Man, you're not right," I said.

"If my mind was a computer chip, I guess there might be a few blips on it," he said.

Hey, I guess I'm lucky my brain was faulty before I even went to Vietnam.

"As someone who travels
with a gallon of tea,
I've got to make a lot of pit stops."

Chapter

19

Iced Tea Glass

BELIEVE IT OR NOT, we actually had pretty good food in the army. There was one cook in Vietnam who baked some of the best cinnamon rolls you could ever want to put in your mouth. He loved to bake, and his cinnamon rolls were humongous. He didn't spare any of Uncle Sam's sugar or cinnamon, either. His cinnamon rolls would melt in your mouth, and we actually cried when he went home.

I worked in the kitchen for a few weeks during basic training at Fort Benning in Columbus, Georgia. I had a crazy buddy I met on the train from Shreveport, Louisiana, and he told me he had the answer to all of our worries about being in the army.

"Hey, we volunteer for everything," he said.

"Look," I said. "Everybody I've talked to told me not to volunteer for nothing. People have warned me about doing something stupid like volunteering."

During our first week of basic training, one of the sergeants walked up to my platoon and said, "I need two volunteers for KP."

I knew KP was kitchen patrol, and I didn't want any part of it. But before I could even move, my buddy had not only his arm up but also mine.

"You idiot," I told him. "This better work out."

Hey, it might have been worse. When I was in Vietnam, one of the sergeants asked my platoon if any of us had experience in radio communications. I nearly raised my hand because I thought I might finally get to see some serious action, but then I thought better of it. Some sucker from Indiana, who was an amateur radio operator, raised his hand instead.

"Good," the sergeant said. "You can dig the hole for the new telephone pole."

For two weeks during boot camp, I helped in the kitchen, mostly peeling potatoes and washing pots and pans. I received a behind-the-scenes look at how the food was prepared and cooked. Hey, it wasn't pretty. Surprisingly, we actually had good meat come into the kitchen. The steaks we were fed were some of the best-looking beef I'd ever seen—at least until the cooks got their hands on them! What the army cooks did to the meat was criminal. Hey, you haven't chewed on a two-dollar steak until you've eaten a New York strip in the army! But the rest of the chow they cooked in the mess hall didn't taste that bad for the most part.

After I was finished with KP, I made the mistake of offering our company cook some advice.

"Hey, if you put a lid on the pan there will be less dust and dirt in your soup," I said.

"You mind your business," he told me. "Your job is to defend South Vietnam."

"That's right," I told him. "My duty is to defend South Vietnam—not eat it!"

Even some of the combat rations the army fed us were pretty edible. Our rations were actually called Meal, Combat, Individual (MCI), but everybody called them C-rations, which was what the army had been feeding its troops since the end of World War II. The MCI was introduced in 1958 and came to us in a cardboard carton, which contained one small flat can, one large can, and two even smaller cans. The cans were stacked on top of each other, so they were easy to carry in your pack.

The M-unit can was a meat-based entrée, which might have been something like beefsteak with potatoes and gravy, beans and wieners, chicken and noodles, chopped ham and eggs, ham and lima beans, or spaghetti with meatballs. The spaghetti was probably my favorite. Crackers, chocolate, hardtack biscuits (everybody called them "John Wayne cookies"), processed cheese, peanut butter, or jam was usually in the B-unit can, and the D-unit can was a dessert, typically something like apricots, peaches, pears, fruit cocktail, pound cake, or applesauce. If you were really unlucky, the D-unit can only contained a couple of pieces of white bread. That was a bad day, Jack!

The army also gave us an accessory pack with each meal, which included a spoon, salt, pepper, sugar, instant coffee, a couple of pieces of chewing gum, and toilet paper, as well as a four-pack of cigarettes and book of twenty matches. I started smoking cigarettes in high school (I have since quit, but I'll tell you more about that later), so I was happy to find them in my accessory pack. Eventually, the U.S. military figured out smoking wasn't healthy for its troops, so the army took cigarettes out of MCIs in 1975. I'll be honest: I was not a happy camper at the time.

Hey, army food wasn't exactly Miss Kay's cooking or fine dining, but you could survive on it and it was better than going hungry.

Of course, I never would have survived twelve months in Vietnam without Momma sending me care packages from home. In one of the first boxes, she mailed me a pair of work boots. There was a Tupperware iced tea cup and a couple of cans of jalapeño peppers in one boot, and a couple of cans of Spam and beans and wieners in the other boot.

I had a small electric cooktop in my hotel room in downtown Can Tho, so I cooked myself late-night meals whenever I was hungry. Shortly after Momma sent me the jalapeño peppers, one of my buddies came into my room. Of course, he'd been drinking whiskey all night and was three sheets to the wind.

"Oh, man!" he said. "Whatcha cookin', Robertson?"

"Hey, get you some of the pork and beans and Spam," I told him. "But you don't want any of these peppers."

"I love hot peppers," he said. "Give me a couple of 'em."

"You don't want any of these," I said. "These are from Louisiana. They get jalapeño in your business!"

He grabbed a couple of peppers anyway. A few seconds later, he ran out of my room looking for water.

Somehow, Momma's iced tea cup stayed with me all the way through Vietnam, and I've carried it with me in my back pocket ever since. I guess if it can make it through the napalm, mustard gas, and rice wine of Vietnam, I'll probably take it to my grave.

Everywhere I go, I carry a gallon of iced tea and my light blue Tupperware cup. Now my cup even has its own Facebook page and Twitter account. Some people might even say my cup has a better personality than my nephew Jase.

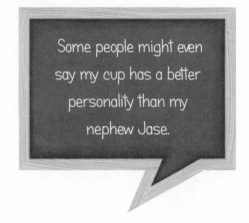

Some people might even say my cup has a better personality than my nephew Jase.

Now, there are plenty of duplicates of my blue Tupperware cup, but there's only one original. It never leaves my sight. One time, a guy handed me a blank check and wanted to buy my iced tea cup.

"Fill in the amount," he said. "Whatever it takes—I want that Tupperware cup."

"It's not for sale," I told him.

I told the guy to go buy his own Tupperware cup, but he insisted he wanted mine. I told him A&E TV wouldn't let me part with it.

During our first season of *Duck Dynasty*, I walked into the Duck Commander warehouse, and one of the workers told me there was a big box for me in the back.

"Are you sure it's for me?" I asked him.

"Oh, yeah, it says Si Robertson on it," he said.

"Hey, put it on the back of the truck," I said.

I took the box home and opened it up. Inside, there was a stainless steel saucepan with a lid, a big boiling pot, and a really nice set of steak knives. I looked at the bottom of the box and there were twelve Tupperware cups.

There was also a letter to me from the chairman and CEO of the Tupperware Brands Corporation in Orlando, Florida.

Apparently, Tupperware cups are making a comeback.

And they have the lovely Merritt Robertson to thank.

"Today, with computers,
if you're dating some little ol' girl online,
you can't even smell her.
Girls smell nice."

Christine and I pose in front of one of our first houses. I probably
asked her to marry me two hundred times before she finally said yes!

Chapter 20

The Woman of
My Dreams

AFTER I LEFT VIETNAM on October 17, 1969, the army transferred me to Fort Devens in Shirley, Massachusetts, which is about fifty-five miles northwest of Boston. I was stationed at Fort Devens for about two years and worked in medical supply. Hey, you want to talk about living in a foreign land. I grew up in the South, and it took me a long time to get used to living in the cold, harsh winters of the Northeast. I'd rarely seen snow in my life, and it seemed like it snowed at Fort Devens eight months out of the year.

Hey, have you ever listened to someone from Boston talk? It sounds like their elementary school teachers went straight from Q to S when teaching them the alphabet. They don't know how to use the letter R! During a weekend pass, I visited Boston with a buddy of mine who was from there. He didn't have a car, so I drove mine. After we visited his parents, he took me to nearby Cambridge, Massachusetts, which is the home of Harvard University. He wanted me to go bar hopping with him to find some college girls. Hey, I figured the Ivy League and I went together like shrimp and grits. I dropped him off outside a bar and he told me, "Pahk the cah at Havad Yad." Of course I had no idea what he said, so I drove around in circles for hours. And some people think *I* talk funny!

People from Boston also used words I'd never heard before. Hey, they refer to shorts as clam diggers and headaches as bangers! They even refer to rubber bands as elastics. Do they use rubber bands to keep up their trousers? I walked into the barbershop on base, and the barber told me he was going to give me a whiffle.

"Are we playing baseball?" I asked him.

The first time I walked into my barrack, I asked a sergeant where I could find some water to drink.

"The bubbler is down the hall," he said.

"The what?" I asked him.

It took me a few minutes to realize he was talking about a water fountain!

Living in the Northeast was definitely a change in scenery for me, but I believe God has a purpose for everything. It didn't take me long to realize he'd sent me to Fort Devens to meet the woman who would become my wife. I met the former Christine Raney for the first time when I was hitchhiking to an off-base nightclub in November 1969. Christine was riding in the car with two of her friends, one of whom I already knew, and they saw me walking down the road. They couldn't have missed me. I was wearing a black leather jacket with a big dragon on the back of it. The dragon practically glowed in the dark. I'd picked the jacket up in

Vietnam. If Christine's friend hadn't recognized me, they probably would have thought I was some rock star.

From the start, Christine didn't like me very much. She thought I was arrogant and full of myself. She even told me, "You think you're the rooster of the walk!"

Christine had been married once before; her husband left her because they didn't think she could bear children. They'd tried to have a baby for a couple of years, but she couldn't get pregnant. Doctors told her she couldn't have children because of an underlying medical condition. Her husband wanted a family, so he left her. When Christine met me, she was still pretty leery about dating men. My buddy had been trying to set her up with some of his friends for months, but she had a long list of demands she wanted in her next boyfriend.

"Well, describe to me the kind of man you want," my buddy told her.

"Okay, here you go," she said. "He has to be six feet to six feet three inches tall with a slender frame. He has to have blue or green eyes and a beautiful smile with dimples. Most importantly, he also has to be smart and have a keen sense of humor and a warm heart."

"I've got just the person for you," he told her.

"There's no way you know anyone with all of those attributes," she said.

Hey, Christine Raney didn't know the real Silas Merritt Robertson. I was eight for eight, Jack!

My buddy set us up on a blind date. Well, at least she was blind going into the date. I knew who I was taking out, but my buddy didn't tell her she was going out with me. He knew how she felt about me after they picked me up hitchhiking. I decided to take Christine to our company's Christmas party at Fort Devens on December 12, 1969. She picked my buddy and me up at our barracks. As soon as Christine saw me, she was convinced it was going to be the worst night of her life. She couldn't remember my name, but she remembered my face. How could anyone forget a face like mine?

Of course, I turned on my charm and we had a great time.

I amazed her with my dancing skills, of course, and we started dating regularly pretty soon thereafter.

Christine said she'd never laughed so hard in her life. I amazed her with my dancing skills, of course, and we started dating regularly pretty soon thereafter.

Christine was born and raised in Kentucky, where her father was a farmer. She loved living in Massachusetts. She'd moved there when she was twenty-one and was working as a seamstress in a factory that made furniture upholstery.

After a couple of years of dating, I was ready to pop the big question. I knew she was the one. My enlistment in the army was about to expire, and I knew I was moving back to Louisiana. I wanted to take Christine with me.

Before I proposed to Christine, I called Momma to tell her the news. I knew Momma and Daddy wouldn't be happy that Christine had been married before. My family didn't believe in divorce. We believed that when you made a vow of marriage, you were supposed to spend the rest of your life with your spouse. I was taught that when you chose a husband or wife, you were making a commitment for the rest of your life. But it wasn't Christine's decision for her first marriage to end.

"Hey, I've got a little news," I told Momma. "I'm fixing to get married. Her name is Christine. She was married before, so I want to make sure you will accept her as your daughter-in-law."

There was a short pause on the other end of the telephone. I was getting a little anxious.

"Yes, I'll accept her," Momma said.

"Good," I said. "This is the woman I'm going to marry. If you can't accept her, I'm not going to be around, either."

"You ought to know better than that," Momma said. "I will accept her."

On April Fools' Day, 1971, I told Christine's best friend that I was going to ask her to marry me. Of course, I was only kidding at the time. Five days later, on the same day I was released from the army, I asked Christine to marry me. Much to my surprise, she told me no.

And then she told me no again—and again and again and again.

Christine didn't want to marry me because she knew she couldn't have children.

"I can't be your broodmare," she said.

"Hey, I'm not like your first husband," I told her. "There are other doctors out there. If God wants us to have children, we'll have children. If he doesn't want us to have children, we'll adopt some kids. I want to marry you."

Finally, after I'd pestered Christine for nearly a full day, she agreed to marry me. We went to see the justice of the peace the next day.

On April 7, 1971, we were married at the courthouse. Because I was leaving the army, the judge even waived the state's requirement of having a five-day waiting period, marriage license, and blood test before a couple could be married.

When we were standing in front of the judge, he said to me, "Son, you just got out of a three-year commitment. Are you sure you want another one?"

"Yes, sir," I told him.

I knew this commitment was for the rest of my life.

Christine and I exchanged our vows and became husband and wife.

"There's some people who got it.
And some people who don't.
Hey, I've always had it!"

My first impression with Christine wasn't much, but I knocked
her socks off once she realized I was a modern-day Fred Astaire!

Chapter
21

Newlyweds

AS SOON AS CHRISTINE and I were married, we jumped into my 1966 Plymouth Fury and drove straight to her parents' home in Kentucky. We were headed to Louisiana, but we stopped there so her parents could meet me. On the way to the courthouse the morning we were married, Christine said I wouldn't stop talking. But she said I barely said a word during the drive from Massachusetts to Kentucky. I guess I was in shock from actually going through with marriage.

We arrived at her parents' home late at night, and I didn't meet them until the next morning.

"Boy, y'all must have been tired," her momma said.

"What were you expecting to hear, Momma?" Christine asked her. "The bedsprings squeaking?"

Thankfully, her parents' house had thick walls.

Hey, Christine was in for a rude awakening when we arrived in Louisiana. I told her she was going to meet my family at a get-together at my brother Harold's house in Ruston, Louisiana. I don't think she realized she was going to meet my entire family. It wasn't like, "Hey, meet Momma and Daddy." It was more like, "Hey, meet my entire family and all of the in-laws."

My grandparents, parents, aunts, uncles, cousins, and second cousins were there, along with practically anyone else who had a spot on our family tree. Christine is a very shy person, and she was worried about meeting my parents, let alone everyone else. There were more than twenty people at the impromptu reunion. She was really taken aback at how loud and competitive we were while playing games like dominoes and solitaire. She barely spoke a word the entire day—not that she had much of a chance to say anything.

Hey, welcome to the Robertson family.

> Christine thought she'd gotten the best of the bunch of Momma's boys.
> Was there ever any doubt?

Fortunately, Christine won over my momma pretty easily. She actually wrote my mother letters thanking her for me. Christine thought she'd gotten the best of the bunch of Momma's boys. Was there ever any doubt? In our first year of marriage, Momma told Christine how happy she was that I'd married her. Momma thought Christine was the perfect wife for me. I was really happy Momma liked her.

Newlyweds

In April 1971, Christine and I moved to Junction City, Arkansas, which is where Phil and Kay were living at the time. It was during Phil's struggles with alcohol and drugs, so it was really a wild time to be around him. As I said earlier, I quit drinking alcohol shortly after I came back from Vietnam. Once I met Christine, I stopped drinking altogether. But Phil was operating a honkytonk and was drinking all the time.

Christine did not like Phil very much in the beginning. In fact, she despised it when I went hunting or fishing with him, which was usually every day. She didn't like the fact that Phil was taking other women on his fishing and hunting trips while he was married to Kay. Phil was my big brother, and I still loved him. But it was very difficult for me to see him go through his struggles. To be honest, Phil was not a very good person until he found Jesus Christ when he was twenty-eight years old. But he repented his sins and is spending the rest of his life sharing God's Word.

Much to my surprise, I had a difficult time after I left the military. When I was in Vietnam, I couldn't wait to get back to the United States. When I was in Massachusetts, I couldn't wait to get back to Louisiana. But once I was closer to home and around my parents, brothers, and sisters again, I was bored out of my mind. I was different from a lot of guys in the military. I put a uniform on every morning when I went to work, but I took it off when I came home. It was more of a job to me than a career. But I liked that I had a lot of free time in the military, which allowed me to hunt and fish. After we moved to Arkansas, I worked a nine-to-five shift in a particleboard factory, and I didn't make much money. I was usually too tired to do the things I liked doing in the outdoors.

In August 1971, Christine and I moved to Ruston, Louisiana. For whatever reason, I decided to go back to school on a GI Bill, which paid my tuition and helped pay for our living expenses as long as I was in college. I took classes at Louisiana Tech University—the administration was more than happy to welcome back one of its honor students—and worked from three o'clock to midnight five days a week. I worked in a broom factory for about two months, but then the owner fired me because his nephew needed a job.

Since I was married, I needed a job to support my wife. The GI Bill didn't cover everything. Fortunately, the Ruston police department was looking to hire a radio operator. Back then there was no such thing as 911, at least not in Ruston, so I was in charge of handling all the emergency calls at night, as well as being a dispatcher for the police officers who were on patrol. You wouldn't believe some of the calls we received! One time, a guy called me and told me his wife was in labor.

"Her contractions are only two minutes apart," he said.

"Is this her first child?" I asked.

"No, you idiot, this is her husband!" he told me.

Hey, another time a guy called me from a pay phone and told me he was having trouble breathing.

"Sir, where are you located?" I asked.

"I'm at the corner of West Kentucky Avenue and South Chautauqua Road," he said.

"Are you asthmatic?" I asked.

"No," he replied.

"Well, what were you doing when you started having trouble breathing?" I asked.

"Running from the police," he said.

It didn't take me long to realize I didn't want to pursue a career in criminal justice. It wasn't very long before I started losing interest in attending college, too. I was enrolled at Louisiana Tech for more than a year, but I just couldn't see myself staying in college for three more years. Five days a week, I was attending classes in the morning, working at night, and studying before and after I went to work. Hey, I figured out I was working a lot less and making a lot more money when I was in the military!

Before too long, Christine could sense my frustration. I'm not an angry person and really don't have much of a temper, but she could see that I wasn't the same happy-go-lucky guy I was when I was in the army. One night after work, she sat me down in our living room.

"Are you happy going to school and working at night?" she asked me.

"No, not really," I said.

"Well, I have a question," she said. "Were you happier in the military than you are here?"

"Yeah, I really enjoyed the military," I said.

"Well, why don't you go back into the army?" she said.

In November 1972, Christine and I drove to the army recruiter's office in Shreveport, Louisiana. They agreed to take me back, and I enlisted that same day. When I signed my contract to go back into the army, I made the recruiter specify that I would spend at least sixteen months at Fort Knox, which is about thirty-five miles from Louisville, Kentucky. I figured Fort Knox was pretty close to Christine's parents, and it would also ensure that the army wouldn't send me back to Vietnam or another foreign country.

Uncle Sam kept his word. We stayed at Fort Knox for sixteen months. On the first day of the seventeenth month, I got my orders to go back overseas.

"This is just the icing
on the tip of the iceberg!"

Hey, the Germans required me to dress pretty sharp for our hunts.
Can you imagine me wearing these duds in Phil's duck blind?

Chapter
22

God's Blessing

ONE OF THE FIRST things I did when I arrived at Fort Knox, Kentucky, was make an appointment for Christine to see a fertility doctor. The military doctor started working with us in December 1972, and he eventually told Christine that he could fix it to where she wouldn't experience any more pain, but he still wasn't sure if we could have children.

A few years earlier, Christine had been diagnosed with Asherman's syndrome, which is a rare condition that causes scarring on the uterus; more than 95 percent of her uterus was covered in scars. The condition can cause infertility and miscarriages and is sometimes very painful. When Christine was working, she often missed at least a couple of days of work every month because she was in excruciating pain.

Christine had surgery in July 1973 to remove the scarring

from her uterus. Fortunately, the procedure eliminated her pain, but we still weren't sure whether we could have children. The doctors told us to keep trying to get pregnant for a year, and we had to closely monitor when she was ovulating. Well, nothing happened in the first nine months after her surgery. The doctors thought everything was fine with Christine, so they wanted to examine me to see if everything was okay. Hey, I didn't want to go see a doctor.

Doctors and I go together like peanut butter and Dijon mustard. We don't get along, Jack! I remember when Momma took me to the doctor for the first time because I was having trouble with my eyes. For a few weeks, everything was really blurry, and I was bumping into walls, tables, chairs, dogs, grizzly bears, and anything else that was in my way.

I was bumping into walls, tables, chairs, dogs, grizzly bears, and anything else that was in my way.

"Mrs. Robertson, your son needs to stop drinking iced tea," the doctor said. "It's bad for his vision."

"Hey, I love iced tea," I said. "I don't care if I go blind. I'm drinking tea, Jack!"

"Well, at least take the spoon out of the cup before you drink it," he said.

Christine was ready to have a baby, so she really wanted me to visit the doctor to find out what was going on. I wanted to have children badly as well, so I agreed to go. After an examination, the doctors thought my sperm count might be low. They handed me a glass jar and told me to bring back a specimen the next day. Now, I'm not going to lie. I didn't feel comfortable doing it. Despite my embarrassment, I agreed to come back with a specimen. The next day, I returned to the doctor's office.

"Where's the sample?" the doctor asked me.

"Hey, I tried to do it," I told him. "But no matter how hard I tried, I couldn't do it. I asked my wife for help, but I still couldn't do it. Then I asked my neighbor to help me, and I even asked my army buddies for assistance. No matter who helped, I couldn't do it."

I looked at the doctor and his face was bright red.

"Hey, none of us could get the lid off the jar," I said.

We found out that my sperm count was very low. Hey, they were Grade A sperm, but there weren't enough of them. The doctors discovered that my body temperature was too warm because I was always wearing tight shorts, kind of like the low-cut ones football coaches used to wear on the sideline. I liked to wear them because they really showcased my legs. To fix the problem, I started wearing boxer shorts and sweatpants. Christine and I went back to trying to have a baby.

In April 1974, when my sixteen-month enlistment at Fort Knox was about to expire, the army notified me that I was being deployed to Baumholder, Germany. The Baumholder post was an old Nazi garrison located in southwest Germany, just east of the French border. Before World War II, the Nazis displaced hundreds of families to build a military training ground that covered nearly thirty thousand acres. During World War II, Baumholder was also the site of a prisoner-of-war camp that housed prisoners from the Soviet Union, Poland, and other countries.

In March 1945, Baumholder surrendered to the Americans

without a fight, and it became a French military outpost. In 1951, the U.S. army took over the outpost and built schools, houses, churches, and warehouses for more than four thousand troops and their families. Until recent military cutbacks, Americans outnumbered the Germans living in Baumholder by nearly three to one. It really was a beautiful area. Rolling hills surrounded Baumholder, and it had bars, dance halls, and music halls from its medieval roots. It was located in the middle of Germany's wine country, and Austria, Belgium, France, Holland, Luxembourg, Switzerland, and the Bavarian Alps were within a few hours' drive. Hey, it was a lot different from Louisiana and Vietnam!

I left for Germany in May 1974, and Christine joined me there about three months later. In December 1974, Christine became very ill. She thought she had the flu. Sharon Sawyer, the woman living next to door to us on the military base, encouraged her to take a pregnancy test.

"I know I'm not pregnant," Christine said. "There's no need to go."

"Do it for me," Sharon told her. "Please do it for me. You never know."

Sharon persuaded Christine to go to the military hospital and take a pregnancy test. Later that day, Sharon asked her to call the hospital to find out the results.

"I'm not even going to call," Christine told her. "I know I'm not pregnant. I know it's going to be negative."

Without Christine's knowing, Sharon called the doctor's office and pretended to be her.

After a few minutes, Christine heard her say: "What do you mean do I want to keep the baby? Of course I'm keeping the baby!"

God's Blessing

Sharon walked into the living room of our apartment and shouted: "We're pregnant! We're pregnant!"

When I found out Christine was pregnant, it was one of the happiest days of my life. I always knew if God wanted us to have children, He would make it happen. If He didn't want us to have kids, we wouldn't have them. I have always left those kinds of things up to the Almighty, and I've always known I've had no control over them.

When I first asked Christine to marry me, she told me, "No, I won't marry you. I've seen you around children and you love them. You need to have kids. You want to have kids."

Even though I would have been perfectly happy adopting kids or living with Christine without them, I'd always wanted children of my own. I loved being around Phil's boys when they were babies, and I really wanted a chance to spread our love with children of our own. As it says in Psalms 113:9: "He settles the childless woman in her home as a happy mother of children. Praise the Lord."

Hey, the next eight months were the most anxious days of my life as I waited for my baby to arrive.

"We are fixing
to have a hootenanny
like you ain't seen in your lifetime!"

Christine and I pose with Trasa when she was only a toddler.
After we had tried for so long to have a baby, her arrival was
one of God's great blessings.

Trasa

ONE OF THE HAPPIEST days of my life was August 30, 1975, when my daughter, Trasa Robertson, was born at a military hospital in Landstuhl, Germany. After going through so many struggles to have a child, Christine and I couldn't have been more excited. We named Trasa after Christine's father, Asa Lee Raney, and she actually has dual citizenship because she was born in Germany while I was stationed there.

From the time Trasa was born, she was Daddy's girl. When Trasa was old enough to crawl, she sat in the foyer of our house every day waiting for me to come home for lunch. She'd sit in my lap while I ate, and then she was waiting in the foyer again at the end of my workday. Her eyes lit up every time I walked in the door, and I don't know that I've ever seen a more beautiful sight.

When Trasa was only a toddler, Christine and I realized that she was an exceptional child. She was an absolute angel until she was three years old, but then she turned into a little devil. Christine took her to the pediatrician on the military base, and the doctor talked to Trasa without her mother in the room. The pediatrician came out and told Christine to put Trasa in preschool because she was bored to death. We put Trasa in preschool for two hours a day, and it really made a difference in her behavior.

Trasa could read before she went to kindergarten. Hey, I told you my stock was Grade A! One day in preschool, the teacher told the class something that wasn't factually correct. My three-year-old daughter stood up and said the right answer. Needless to say, the teacher didn't like being corrected by a toddler.

Trasa was always a very curious child. When we lived in Germany, I still liked to go squirrel hunting. I'd kill five or six squirrels and bring them home to cook. Trasa was probably only five years old at the time, but I had her hold the squirrels' legs while I skinned them. As I was gutting the squirrels, she would always ask what the organs were.

"What's that?" she asked.

"That's its kidneys," I told her.

"What's that?" she asked again.

"That's its heart," I said.

She was fascinated by the anatomy of a squirrel, while most girls her age would have been completely grossed out. Squirrels are my favorite game to eat, and Trasa loves eating them, too. When she started dating her future husband in college, they were sitting on a park bench, watching squirrels run around in the grass.

"Oh, I'd love to have a rock and hit them and then take them home and cook them," Trasa said.

Trasa's boyfriend looked at her like she was nuts and asked, "What are you talking about?"

"That's the best meat you'll ever eat," she told him.

Hey, that's my girl. She's a chip off the old block.

When Trasa was eight years old, a military psychologist on the base tried to tell us how to treat her because she was so intellectually gifted. But we wanted our daughter to be normal, so we treated her like any other kid. To this day, Trasa thanks us for not treating her like she was different.

When Trasa was growing up, if Christine or I needed to punish her, we would take her books away. She always begged us to take away something else, like the TV or dessert, but we took her books away because we knew how much she loved to read and learn. Eventually, we even had to put a time limit on how long she could read. If Trasa didn't have a book in her hand, we thought something was wrong with her. Sometimes I would ask her, "Hey, why don't you have a book in your hand? Are you sick?"

Because Trasa was so intellectually gifted, she never had many friends growing up. In fact, she was very isolated and kind of a loner until middle school. But then Trasa made two friends in the sixth grade, and the girls made a world of difference for her. One of the girls knew how to wear makeup, and Christine asked her to teach Trasa how to use it. The girls went shopping together, and Trasa started buying clothes that the other teenagers were wearing. She never worried about her appearance as much as she did about her brain. More than anything, those girls taught Trasa how to be a teenager.

Along the way, I learned that raising a teenager is about as hard as trying to nail Jell-O to a tree. I tried to do the best I could do and offered Trasa and her friends advice whenever they needed it. Hey, I'd rather they learned from me than from their friends or somebody on TV. I remember one of the girls' mothers asking me if I minded her daughter being at our house all the time.

"Hey, I better ask you this: do you mind her being over here all the time?" I said. "Because if they bring up a topic, there is nothing taboo in this house. If they want to ask me about sex, I'm going to tell them how it is."

One night, I warned the girls about the dangers of drinking alcohol.

I called the three girls into our kitchen, where I filled one glass with water and another one with whiskey. Then I placed a worm in each of the glasses. The worm in the water lived, while the worm in the whiskey shriveled up and died.

"What does that tell you?" I asked them.

"Well, I won't have worms like a dog if I drink alcohol," Trasa said.

It wasn't exactly the lesson I was going for.

Sometimes Trasa's sleepovers didn't go so smoothly, either. One night, Christine left me with a handful of ten-year-old girls while she went to a friend's house to play bridge.

"Whatever you do, do not let these girls leave this house," Christine said.

A couple of hours later, one of Trasa's friends came downstairs.

"I need to go home," she said.

"Nope, you're not going anywhere," I told her. "Go back upstairs."

A few minutes later, the girl was standing in the living room again.

"Mr. Robertson, I really need to go home," she said. "I was supposed to be home an hour ago."

"Hey, I'm under strict orders from headquarters," I said. "Nobody leaves this house."

About an hour later, there was a knock at the front door. It was a lady who lived down the street.

"Is my daughter here?" she asked.

"Nope," I said. "I haven't seen her."

Then the little girl stuck her head around the corner.

"Momma, I've been trying to come home," she said. "But he won't let me leave!"

In October 1992, the army transferred me back to the United States. Trasa was in her senior year of high school, and we made the difficult decision to leave our seventeen-year-old daughter with coworkers and friends in Germany. I didn't want to be away from my daughter for a year, but I knew it was the best thing for her. We'd always talked about what happened to me during my senior year of high school, when my parents moved from Dixie, Louisiana, to Gonzales, Louisiana. I had to move schools during the middle of my senior year and graduated with people I didn't know. I was determined not to do that to my children. We talked to Trasa about it, and she understood the situation and was very grateful we were leaving her behind. It was a very long year without her.

Trasa was attending Zweibrucken American High School in Zweibrucken, Germany, which was located on a United States Air Force base. The school also served the children of troops stationed at two nearby army facilities. It was an exceptional school, and she received a fantastic education. When Trasa graduated from high school in 1993, she received a Presidential Scholarship to Texas

A&M University in College Station, Texas. In high school she was named a student delegate to the United Nations and visited the Hague in the Netherlands. As a National Merit Scholar she was invited to the White House in Washington, DC, where she met First Lady Hillary Clinton. We couldn't have been more proud of her.

She also excelled at Texas A&M. During Trasa's sophomore year of college, one of her close friends was working as a fashion model. She invited Trasa to attend one of her photo shoots, and the modeling agency became interested in Trasa. She eventually became a model in advertisements around the country. I was so happy for her. Until Trasa was fifteen, she never felt like she was pretty. But she really blossomed by the end of high school. As a child, Trasa wore Coke-bottle eyeglasses. When Trasa was eight years old, we were told she would probably be blind by the time she was twenty-one. I told her we wouldn't worry about it, and God would take care of everything. It was a hereditary condition. Christine's father was legally blind in one eye until he had laser surgery when he was much older. Fortunately, Trasa's vision gradually improved, and she was able to wear contact lenses by the time she was fifteen.

Trasa graduated from Texas A&M in 1997. She took a year off from school between her junior and senior years because she was starting to get burned out. She spent a year working as a model and waitressing and really enjoyed it, then returned to Texas A&M the next year to finish her bachelor's degree. She was offered a scholarship to attend law school at Southern Methodist University in Dallas, but turned it down; she had other plans for her life.

Trasa met her future husband, Kyle Cobern, during her freshman year at Texas A&M. He is nine years older than Trasa, and they've been married for seventeen years now. Kyle is perfect for our daughter, and that's really all any parent could ever want. Trasa now has four sons—Brady Silas, Caden, Jaxon, and McCrae—and she absolutely loves being a mother. She teaches middle school in Hurst, Texas, and loves what she's doing. I couldn't be more proud of and happy for her.

Looking back now, it's amazing how much the good Lord has blessed us. For the first four years of our marriage, Christine and I weren't sure we could have children. But as I said earlier, I put it in God's hands. I knew I had to have faith in the Lord. As it says in Matthew 21:21, "Jesus replied, 'Truly I tell you, if you have faith and do not doubt, not only can you do what was done to the fig tree, but also you can say to this mountain, "Go, throw yourself into the sea," and it will be done.'"

A couple of months after Trasa was born, Christine returned to her doctor for a routine checkup. She asked him if we could have another child.

"If I'd seen you before your first child, I would have told you that you could never have children," he said. "If you had one, I don't see why you can't have another one."

I knew if the Lord wanted us to have another child, then Trasa would soon have a brother or sister.

"You can't tell by looking at me, but I'm a comedy man!"

I was a big fan of muscle cars when I was younger.
This beauty required nearly as much oil as gas!

Chapter
24

Like Father, Like Son

CHRISTINE WASN'T PREGNANT FOR ten days before she started having problems with our second baby. I like to joke that our son, Scott, was trouble before he was even born. Scott was born at a military hospital at Lackland Air Force Base in San Antonio, Texas, on December 18, 1977.

After we returned to the United States from Germany in July 1977, I was stationed at Fort Lee, which is near Petersburg, Virginia, and Christine and Trasa went to stay with her parents in Kentucky. When the army transferred me to Fort Polk in Leesville, Louisiana, in September 1977, Christine's parents brought them down to live with me. Two weeks later, Christine started having serious problems.

One morning, I woke up to go squirrel hunting. Hey, it was the first time I'd been back in Louisiana in a long time, and I couldn't wait to go shoot the long-tailed critters! But for whatever reason, Christine didn't want me to go hunting. "Why not?" I asked her.

"I don't have a reason," she said. "I just have a feeling that you're not supposed to go."

"That's not good enough," I said. "I'm going to shoot me some squirrels."

When I came home from hunting, I found a note on our front door. Christine was at the hospital because of complications from her pregnancy, and Trasa was down the street at the preacher's house. Doctors told Christine there was a serious problem with her pregnancy and broke the devastating news that her fetus would probably die. But a month went by and Christine didn't miscarry, so the doctors took another ultrasound in October 1977. The fetus was still alive, and the doctors decided that when Christine was seven months pregnant, they would hospitalize her until our baby was born.

On the day after Thanksgiving Day 1977, Christine was admitted to the military hospital at Fort Polk, where she was supposed to stay for the next three months. But on December 8, 1977, Christine started having contractions. The next day, she was flown to San Antonio because there was an experimental drug there that doctors believed might be able to stop her contractions. Our baby wasn't due until February 5, 1978. If the baby was born in December, there was a good chance he wouldn't survive.

On December 17, Christine started hemorrhaging and doctors couldn't stop the bleeding. They delivered our son, Scott, the next day. I was at Fort Polk when Christine started hemorrhaging, and the doctors called me and told me I needed to jump on the next flight to San Antonio. When I walked off the elevator at the hospital, I saw Christine walking down the hall. I looked at her and figured she hadn't delivered the baby yet.

"I've already had the baby," she said. "Come on, let's go down and see him."

"Hey, get out of here," I said. "You haven't had the baby."

"Trust me," she said. "I had the baby. Let's go see your son."

Scott was in critical care because he was seven weeks premature. You couldn't really see him because there were so many tubes and wires sticking out of him. For years, Christine joked that Scott was the ugliest baby she'd ever seen! When Scott was born, Christine kind of went into a shell because she was convinced he wouldn't survive. It was a very scary time for us. The doctors told us the biggest factor on Scott's side was that he weighed five pounds, thirteen ounces when he was born. Even though Scott was born nearly two months premature, he was still a pretty good-sized baby.

For years, Christine joked that Scott was the ugliest baby she'd ever seen!

When Scott was only three days old, I left to spend the night at a friend's house. Before Christine went to bed, she liked to go down and see him in the neonatal intensive care unit. She liked to rub his stomach and tell him she loved him. But on the third night, she walked into the ICU and the nurses told her she needed to go back to her room. All of the nurses were around Scott. She knew something was wrong, so she called me and told me to come back to the hospital.

Before I got to the hospital, doctors operated on Scott because his liver wasn't functioning properly. His bilirubin levels were critically high, and the doctors didn't discover the problem until he was three days old. Bilirubin is a brownish-yellow substance found in bile. It is produced when the liver breaks down old red blood cells. Bilirubin is then removed from the body through feces and urine. When bilirubin levels are high, jaundice causes a baby's skin and the whites of its eyes to turn yellow.

Scott was given a blood transfusion, and thankfully the Lord healed him.

When I arrived at the hospital that night, a doctor apologized to me for operating on my son without my permission.

"Hey, did he need it?" I asked.

"If we hadn't operated on him, he would have died," the doctor said.

"Then no apology is necessary," I said.

Well, we found out a few years later that Scott's high bilirubin levels had damaged part of his brain. Scott was suicidal from the time he was about five years old. His behavior was really erratic as a child. When Scott would get tired, he would throw his arms out and fall backward. When we were hunting hogs in Germany one time, Scott fell on the ground, which concerned the Germans who were hunting with us. "Hey, he does that all the time," I told them. Scott would fall down wherever we went; he did it in stores, in school, and while we were walking down the sidewalk.

I never realized my son had serious problems. I don't know if I'm hardheaded, I'm stubborn, or I just wanted to overlook it, but Christine kept telling me Scott had real problems.

"Well, hey, then I had problems, too," I said. "All kids have problems."

It took me a while to realize Scott needed help. When Scott was angry, he was out of control and did a lot of damage. The tipping point came when he was eleven years old. He came home from school, and Christine could sense that he was very tense. His bedroom was his safe haven. He had to learn to never get angry outside of his bedroom. Well, Scott walked into his bedroom that day, closed the door, and proceeded to destroy everything. When it was finally quiet, Christine went into the room. Scott was getting ready to jump out a second-story window. I don't know if the fall would have killed him, but it was straight down. Christine grabbed Scott and pulled him back into his room.

"I can't go on," Scott said. "I can't do it. I just can't. You're my mother. You're supposed to help me. Make the pain go away."

It broke our hearts. Christine called the military hospital and we took him there the next morning. We met with a new military psychiatrist, and Scott was his very first patient. The psychiatrist told us there was a new drug on the market, and he wanted Scott to take it. The psychiatrist diagnosed Scott with having an attention disorder, hyperactivity, and a behavioral disorder.

The psychiatrist told us we wouldn't see the effects of the new drug for ten to fourteen days. But on the third day, Scott got himself out of bed and walked into the kitchen for breakfast with a big smile on his face. We didn't know who he was! From that day forward, Scott became a typical child. He never lost his temper and rarely had mood swings. He continued to see a psychiatrist until he was seventeen years old, but he never had serious emotional or behavioral problems again. We eventually figured out Scott was suffering from Asperger's syndrome, which is a form of autism.

The military psychiatrist saved my son's life. There's no doubt in my mind that God had a hand in our finding the doctor who could control Scott's disorders. It was another example of God taking care of us. It always seemed like when we desperately needed someone to help us, like when we were trying to get pregnant, God pointed us in the right direction and put people in our lives who could fix our problems. As it says in Proverbs 3:5–6, "Trust in the Lord with all your heart and lean not on your own understanding; in all your ways submit to him, and he will make your paths straight."

Eventually, Scott became a good student and graduated from Paint Rock Valley High School in Princeton, Alabama, in 1996. From the time Scott was a young boy, all he ever wanted to do was join the army. Christine and I tried to talk him out of it and told him he could find a better career, but he wouldn't listen. Christine even pointed out things about the military he wouldn't like, such as authority and obeying orders. Even though Scott was a good student, he liked to argue with his teachers. We told him he couldn't argue with his superior officers in the military.

We never thought the army would accept Scott because of his medical history. When the military recruiters came to Scott's high school, he talked with representatives of the navy, marine corps, and air force. He didn't talk to the army. As soon as Scott told the recruiters about his behavioral conditions, they told him he wouldn't pass the physical exams to join the military. We thought that was the end of it and Scott would find something else to do with his life.

As soon as Scott graduated from high school, he left to visit Trasa in Texas. Scott called his mother about a week later and told her he'd enlisted in the army.

"I have one question," Christine said. "How did you manage that with your medical history?"

"Don't ask, don't tell," he said.

"Scott, that doesn't apply to your medical history," she said.

"Well, they didn't ask, and I didn't tell them," he said.

Scott joined the army and went to basic training at Fort Jackson in Columbia, South Carolina, in November 1997. He completed advanced individual training at Fort Eustis in Virginia. It was the same exact training I had when I joined the army. When Scott tells me things about the army, it's like I'm reliving my experiences. He even had a superior officer named Doc just like me! I always tell him, "Scott, didn't you learn anything? I always told you, don't be like your dad!"

Scott and his wife, Marsha, have four boys—Ethan, twins Connor and Logan, and Wyatt—and live at Fort Eustis. They had Wyatt in July 2013, giving Christine and me eight grandsons. I'll have my own baseball team if Trasa or Scott has one more child! Ethan was Marsha's son from her first marriage, but Scott adopted him last year. Ethan was signing his name as Ethan Robertson at school, and his teachers kept telling him he couldn't do it. "Oh, yes, I can," Ethan said. "Scott Robertson is my dad."

One night, Ethan asked Marsha what would happen to him if anything happened to her.

"Well, Connor and Logan will stay with Scott, and Scott would have to go to court to get you," she said.

"I don't like the sound of that," Ethan said.

Last Christmas, Scott and Marsha wrapped a birth certificate with Ethan's name change and a duck call engraved with his new name and put it under the Christmas tree.

Christine and I received another grandson that Christmas, and it was the best present of our lives.

"Work hard, nap hard.

Hey, that's what I always say, Jack!"

Sleepwalking

AFTER SCOTT WAS BORN, we spent four more years at Fort Polk, where I worked with the Fifth Aviation Battalion, which is an air ambulance detachment of helicopters. Hey, I learned that flying a helicopter is really no different than riding a bicycle. It's just a lot harder to put baseball cards in the spokes. My kids really liked living at Fort Polk, and I was happy to be back in Louisiana. But Christine was never very fond of the place. The base was located in the middle of a swamp and the mosquitoes were bad. When Christine came to pick me up from work on the base one day, there was an alligator sitting in the middle of the road. That might have been the straw that broke the llama's back. In 1982, the army transferred me to Zweibrucken, Germany. When we boarded a plane to fly to Frankfurt, Germany, Christine told me, "You'll never get me to live in this state again!" I knew she was serious. I loved being closer to my parents, brothers, and sisters, but Christine was never very close to her siblings. Her family wasn't as close as mine, so she didn't realize how important living in Louisiana was for me.

During the first two years we were living back in Germany, Christine became very depressed and was really battling her emotions. Scott was about three years old at the time—before we'd gotten him help—and I think Scott's problems were weighing on her mind. She felt guilty because she didn't know how to help him. She was always upset. I didn't yet understand the gravity of the situation. I don't think I wanted to accept that my son had serious emotional problems; I wanted him to be like every other kid. But Christine knew something was wrong with Scott, and she wasn't a very happy person for two years. Finally, I came home from work one day and told her, "Get help or I'm gone. I'm not going to live like this."

After we both calmed down, Christine told me that whenever she pictured herself being old and gray, she thought of herself sitting in a rocking chair with me sitting next to her. Christine told me she couldn't see herself living without me, so she agreed to go to a psychiatrist to get help. In order to get the help Christine needed, she had to move back to the United States with our kids.

In 1984, Christine and our kids flew back to the United States and moved in with Christine's parents in Kentucky. We shipped our furniture back with them, so I lived in the barracks on base. It was like I was in boot camp all over again, living like a bachelor in the military. Christine started seeing a psychiatrist, and thankfully the doctor was able to help her. During their sessions, Christine revealed that a relative had sexually molested her when she was younger. Christine never told her parents about it and internalized the painful memories for many years.

Talking about her past and getting the issues out in the open really helped Christine. It was like a great burden had been lifted from her shoulders, and it helped me understand what she was dealing with. The psychiatrist told Christine that any relationship with God as its center has a better chance of being mended. We each knew we needed one another. As it says in Ecclesiastes 4:9–11, "Two are better than one, because they have a good return for their labor: If either of them falls down, one can help the other up. But pity anyone who falls and has no one to help them up. Also, if two lie down together, they will keep warm. But how can one keep warm alone?"

Christine wasn't the only one with problems when we were moved to Germany for a second time, although my issues seemed trivial in comparison. I was having a lot of problems at work; one of the colonels in Germany just didn't like me for whatever reason. For an entire year, I sat behind my desk and did nothing. I did not have a specified job, but I still had to show up for work every day. Somehow, I upset a bunch of my superiors by doing my job, so they took my job away from me. By exiling me to a desk, my superiors thought I would quit, request a transfer, or do something wrong that would enable them to get rid of me.

But what they didn't know about Silas Merritt Robertson is that I'm perfectly content doing nothing. I showed up every day wearing spit-shined boots, a pressed uniform, and a big smile on my face. I kicked my feet up on my desk and rubbed it in their faces for eight hours a day for twelve months. On most days, I put my head down and slept for a few hours. Hey, I can sleep anywhere. Look here, napping is just like hunting. If I walk through the warehouse when I'm at work, I look over, and there's the perfect spot. Boom! I'm asleep.

I learned to sleep and ignore my surroundings when I was young. When I got past my bed-wetting stage, I moved into the bedroom with my three brothers. There was always a lot of noise in the bedroom because there were four boys sleeping in the same bed. I never slept with a pillow over my head because I was afraid the fairies would take all of my teeth! Sometimes I slept in a sleeping bag on the floor; I was a human tortilla. I tried to sleep with an electric blanket one time, and I even plugged it into a toaster to make it warmer. But then I kept popping up out of bed all night!

I've always loved to sleep. Hey, like I always say: work hard; nap hard. Napping is my favorite thing to do. In fact, I believe it should be our national pastime. Hey, when I'm napping, I might be dreaming about ducks, beavers, squirrels, Stevie Nicks, or anything else. When I'm asleep, it's just my mind and me. Everybody should take a nap once a day. It's a medical fact. Work! Work! Work! Nobody takes time to stop and smell the roses anymore. Hey, doctors have proven that daytime naps improve your memory and help you remember important facts. I guess that's why my mind is like *Encyclopaedia Britannica*.

Look, I've never had a problem falling asleep or staying asleep. When I was younger, I was asleep in my bed at my parents' log house. Phil was in the bed with me, and he heard something scurrying outside. Phil grabbed his rifle, opened the window, and laid the rifle across my chest to steady it. He fired a shot at a squirrel and missed. He missed the squirrel two more times, but I never woke up. Phil said I lay there snoring, while he fired three shots out the window!

Sleepwalking

When I was a little bit older, my sister Judy started dating when she was in high school. One night, Judy came home with her boyfriend, who was a football player at North Caddo High School. When Judy and the boy opened the front door to our house, I was standing in the living room, looking right at them. I was sleepwalking! Then I bolted out the front door and took off running down the road. The boy realized I was asleep, so he took off running after me. He chased me for two miles before he caught me. The next day, the boy came to our house. He told me, "Man, I thought I was fast. But I couldn't keep up with you!"

It's amazing what some people can do when they're sleepwalking. There is a nurse in North Wales who draws and paints works of art while he's sleeping. A woman in England woke up one night at two A.M. and found her husband mowing the grass while he was naked! Tragically, an electrician in Wisconsin sleepwalked out of his house wearing only his underwear and a shirt and froze to death before he woke up. Hey, I do all sorts of things while I'm sleepwalking. I've run marathons, washed the dishes, vacuumed the house, cleaned my rifles, and prepared a big pot of gumbo. Christine never wakes me up when I'm sleepwalking because she says it's when I'm most productive! Hey, what do you call a sleepwalking nun? A roamin' Catholic, Jack!

Obviously, it didn't take the army very long to figure out that I wouldn't have any problems sleeping through twelve months on the job. Fortunately, I was able to get back into the good graces of Uncle Sam when a new colonel was assigned to our unit. I was transferred back to the U.S. in 1985 and rejoined my family at Fort Bragg in Fayetteville, North Carolina. Being reunited with Christine and my kids was one of the happiest days of my life.

And I couldn't wait to climb into my own bed again.

"These boys packed so much stuff, hey, they could survive a zombie nuclear a-poca-liss."

Serving in the Army for so long allowed me to hunt all over the country and the world. I dropped this buck near Fort Bragg, North Carolina.

Chapter 26

Mass Murder

ONE OF THE BEST things about being in the military is that I was able to hunt all over the world. I've hunted in Germany as well as Alabama, Kentucky, Louisiana, North Carolina, and Texas. Hey, you haven't hunted until you've sat in a deer stand with artillery shells firing over your head! That's exactly what happened to me at Fort Bragg, and it didn't take me long to find another deer stand, Jack! Believe me, it's a sound you'll never forget!

When I was stationed in Zweibrucken, Germany, I had a buddy who was the hunting instructor for the area. If you were in the American military and wanted to hunt in Germany, you had to go through eight weeks of classes to learn the German traditions and hunting regulations. Until you were certified, you weren't allowed to hunt there. When my buddy went back to the United States, he talked me into taking over as the hunting instructor. I couldn't speak German very well, but a lot of the local hunters liked me and allowed me to hunt on their land.

Hunting in Germany was a little different than how we do it in the United States. Most hunting clubs in the U.S. lease land to hunt for ducks, deer, birds, and other game, but in Germany you actually lease the animal rights for a certain piece of property. A lot of the hunters sold what they killed to restaurants to recoup some of the money they were paying to hunt. If an American soldier killed a deer or hog on someone's property, we had to pay the rights holder money to keep the meat. We hunted for roe deer, wild hogs, foxes, birds, and German *hasen,* or hares.

German hunts were more like a big party. They were very big events, including an elaborate posthunt meal and, of course, a lot of beer drinking. Sometimes I was in charge of bringing the noon meal. I usually had the mess hall cook a big pot of chili or beef stew, but sometimes I'd cook the Germans barbecued pork or another American dish.

The first year I taught the hunting course, seven Americans were in my class, and I took them hunting when the course was over. On our first hunt, six of the Americans killed a roe deer, which is a lot smaller than the deer we have over here. Roe deer typically weigh between thirty and seventy-five pounds, and they have reddish bodies with short, erect antlers. They're good to eat, but they're just not very big. Germany is about the size of Oregon, and they kill over six hundred thousand roe deer every year. They're everywhere!

One of the great things about hunting in Germany was that it didn't get dark until about ten o'clock at night. If you went deer hunting, you hunted all day long. On the first hunt, one of the Americans who killed a roe deer wanted to keep the meat, but he wanted me to clean it because he didn't know how. We paid for the deer and gutted it in the woods. By the time we got back to the apartment complex where I lived, it was close to midnight.

"Well, it's late and I don't feel like fooling with it tonight," I told him. "I'm going to hang it up in the basement."

I tied a rope around a water pipe and hung the deer from the ceiling. I put a plastic tub under the deer so blood wouldn't drip all over the floor. It was cold in the basement during the wintertime, so I decided to go to work the next morning and then clean the deer when I came home.

Hey, when I came home from work the next day, there were four military police cars and another five German police cars sitting outside my apartment complex. There was even an emergency medical wagon sitting in the parking lot. "What in the world is going on?" I asked myself.

When I walked up to my apartment, one of my neighbors told me, "Hey, there's been a mass murder in our apartment building!"

"Get out of here!" I told him. "A mass murder?"

"Hey, I'm serious," he said. "There's blood everywhere!"

Immediately, I ran to my apartment to make sure Christine and the kids were okay. They were fine, so I went back downstairs to see what was going on. I saw a German doctor I'd been hunting with the day before.

"What's going on?" I asked him.

"Oh, they found a roe deer in the basement," he said.

"All of this for a roe deer?" I said. "What are you doing here?"

"They called me here to determine the cause of death," he said.

"Well, what did you tell them?" I asked.

"I told them it looked like a thirty-aught-six to me," he said.

"You're exactly right," I said.

Well, a woman in my apartment building had gone down to the basement that afternoon to do her laundry. She saw the deer hanging from the ceiling and freaked out. The crazy woman ran out of the basement screaming, "Mass murder! Mass murder!"

Fortunately, I was able to talk my way out of the predicament. The police even let me keep the evidence.

Hunting roe deer was a lot of fun because they would appear out of nowhere at any time. They're so small that they love hiding in tall grass. You would be walking through a field and roe deer would start popping up everywhere.

One time when we were hunting, one of my buddies killed the first wild hog on the property in about twelve years. It was near the end of the day, and there were three of us hunting. I put one guy in the stand and told him he couldn't shoot anything but a fox or pig. The other guy and I went down to a different stand to find a deer. The guy with me hadn't been hunting before, and I kept telling him he was making too much noise.

"Hey, you have to be still," I told him. "If you'll be quiet, we'll kill a deer in about fifteen minutes. I'm listening to the deer eat corn right in front of us. When they're done eating corn, they're going to walk out here and eat some grass."

Well, he never sat still and the deer never walked in front of us. Right before dark, I heard gunfire. Boom! Boom! Then I heard something big fall to the ground.

"Well, either that's a giant fox or that sucker has killed a pig," I said.

We climbed out of our stand and walked toward him. He'd killed a one-hundred-and-fifty-pound pig.

"You haven't gutted him?" I asked.

"No, I was afraid I'd mess it up," he said.

"Boys, here's rule number one in hunting: if you're going to shoot something, you have to learn to clean it," I said.

I gutted the hog in the woods and we carried it back to my Mitsubishi Montero. We drove to the landowner's house and knocked on the door. His wife answered and told us he wasn't there. He was at a guesthouse on the north side of town. When we found the owner, he couldn't believe we'd killed a pig on his property. Being in Germany, we had to discuss the hunt over a couple of pitchers of beer. The owner kept the hog, but he gave my buddy its teeth as a trophy.

Boys, here's rule number one in hunting: if you're going to shoot something, you have to learn to clean it.

The landowners in Germany were very particular about what you could shoot on their property. They didn't like us shooting the biggest hogs. During one hunt, I noticed a hole that looked like a big horseshoe in the middle of tall brush. It was actually a trail where hogs had been running. A few minutes later, I heard dogs barking and it was getting louder. The dogs were running toward me! All of the sudden, the big hole in the brush was gone. A hog stuck its head through and kept running right at me. I didn't think it was going to stop, so I grabbed my gun. The hog came within about three feet of me, but then it turned around and ran back into the hole. My sergeant major was with me and was yelling, "Can I shoot him? Can I shoot him?"

"No, he's too big," I said.

The hog probably weighed more than three hundred pounds and had huge tusks sticking out of the sides of its snout. It was pretty, but it was too big to shoot. A few minutes later, guns started going off, and I saw a forty-pound hog running my way. I looked through the scope of my rifle and saw two big oak trees. If the hog ran between the trees, I thought I had one chance to shoot it—if someone else didn't get it first. When the hog hit my scope, I fired and the hog flipped in the air. The Germans blew their horns, signaling that the hunt was over. One of the Germans came down and asked everyone who shot it. About five guys claimed it, but I told him I was the last one to shoot when it fell. They gave the hog to my colonel, which was probably a good thing.

It was always fun to see the spread after a German hunt. There was such a variety of game. There was usually an elk, four or five roe deer, twelve hogs, a couple of pheasants, and a bunch of rabbits. You have to understand that a German *hase* isn't much smaller than a roe deer. They're the biggest rabbits I've ever seen! Whenever we went rabbit hunting, the Germans always warned us not to confuse a roe deer with a rabbit. But it was easy to do because they are so similar in size.

The first time I went rabbit hunting, I was convinced they had bulletproof fur! The Germans liked to shoot over-under shotguns, and I watched four of them fire at the same rabbit. Every time one of them shot twice, I saw fur fly, but the rabbit kept running. As the rabbit got closer, I told myself the rabbit wasn't going to get by me. When it got close to me, the dogs were just about to catch it. The Germans were screaming, "Don't shoot the dog! Don't shoot the dog!" I fired my gun. Boom! It was a head shot and the rabbit flipped. The dog was so close it caught the rabbit in the air.

Mass Murder

I'm not sure what would have happened if I'd accidentally shot the German's dog. Those Germans loved their dogs. I've never had much success with hunting dogs—except for standarad poodles—but the Germans train their dogs meticulously. Sometimes when I walked into a restaurant in Germany, dogs would be sitting next to a table while their masters ate steaks. The dogs didn't move and didn't have an ounce of slobber on their mouths. That wouldn't happen in Louisiana. At Phil's house, Miss Kay's dogs usually eat steak before we do!

One of the most ferocious dogs I've ever seen was in Germany—and it weighed only ten pounds! It was only a puppy, but it had razor-sharp teeth. Before we went hunting one morning, a couple of dogs started fighting. The little dog had latched on to a German shorthaired pointer's ear and wouldn't let go. I thought, *Man, that dog's tough. He's a buzz saw with teeth!* When the hunt started, dogs and pigs were running everywhere. All of the sudden, I saw a two-hundred-pound hog running toward me. The pig kept shaking its head. The little dog had latched on to its ear and wouldn't let go! A couple of hours later, the little dog ripped the ears right off of a rabbit!

It's a good things rabbits have good eyesight from eating so many carrots. If that rabbit had needed glasses, it would have been in trouble!

"I live by my own rules (reviewed, revised, and approved by my wife) . . . but still my own rules."

Trasa poses with one of her prom dates.
Once she lost her glasses and gained some confidence,
my daughter was a beauty!

Semiretirement

I WAS STATIONED IN GERMANY three times for a total of nearly eight years while I served in the army. During my last deployment to Germany, the army informed me it didn't need me anymore. In 1992, Congress trimmed the military budget by more than $278 million, and I was part of the cuts. After serving for more than twenty-four years, Uncle Sam forced me into retirement on January 31, 1993. The army told me to hit the road, Jack!

Christine and I moved to Hollytree, Alabama, which is located in the northern part of the state, not far from the Tennessee border. Christine and I really enjoyed living in the mountains in Germany, and the Appalachian Mountains in north Alabama were beautiful as well. We rented a house from an army friend of mine for about a year, and then we bought a place of our own and lived there for four more years. Trasa was in college, but Scott was still living with us and attended high school in Alabama.

Hey, you know what I didn't do after I retired from the military? I didn't shave. After shaving my face for more than two decades while I was in the army, I threw away my razors, Jack! Phil already had a long beard, and most of the Duckmen who were hunting with him on a regular basis had long, thick beards. Facial hair helps hide your pale skin from ducks. You might as well be wearing spotlights if you get into a duck blind with a clean-shaven face. The ducks will see you from a mile away! I've learned over the last several years that a beard helps camouflage your face and keeps you warm during the winter.

Hey, it's tough being this good-looking.

Hey, you want to talk about fifty shades of gray? I have an entire range of hues in my beard nowadays. Hey, it's tough being this good-looking.

Our house in Alabama was located in the mountains, and our property actually had about four levels from where rock had busted through the earth. It was a great hunting ground. There was an abundance of game and so many places to hide. I could walk on an upper level of rock and look down and see everything. One day, I was deer hunting and thought I heard a buck rubbing its antlers on a tree. But when I looked down, I saw about forty turkeys. I crawled closer to get a better look, but the scout saw me and started chirping. The turkeys took off running! I never figured out where the turkeys came from or where they went! Turkeys also liked to climb into a pine tree in my yard. Four turkeys climbed the tree, with one facing east, one west, one north, and one south. The rest of the turkeys slept under the tree, while the four in the tree stood guard.

We also had two giant pear trees about ten yards from our house. One day, a doe with two fawns walked into our yard to eat pears that had fallen to the ground. The deer gorged themselves on the pears for about thirty minutes. Every time one of the deer moved, it farted! The deer ate so many pears it looked like their bodies were going to explode! Their bellies were so bloated. I'd never seen a deer with so much gas! Christine, Scott, and I sat on the front porch laughing at them. When the deer finally left, they sounded like a train leaving our yard!

Now, I told you I don't like snakes, and I don't care if they're venomous or nonvenomous. If you bring a snake close to me, you're going to get hurt! I had a garden in our backyard in Alabama that was surrounded by waist-high grass. One day, I was out picking tomatoes, cucumbers, and peppers from our garden, and our wiener dog ran into the weeds. As soon as the dog yelped, I knew what had happened to it. A rattlesnake had bitten the dog. I took the dog inside our house, and I saw the fang marks while Christine was holding it. We took the dog to the vet, but he said he couldn't do anything because it was too much venom for such a little dog. The vet ended up putting our dog down.

About two weeks later, I was driving back to our house and saw a bunch of people gathered around a barn by my driveway. I looked and saw a big rattlesnake lying in the middle of the road. I drove my truck over the snake about ten times. I put it in reverse, slammed on the brakes, and made sure the snake was as flat as a pancake! When it was dead, I saw that the snake had about ten rattles and a button. It was huge! I knew it was the snake that killed my dog. One of my neighbors asked me if I wanted the rattles.

"No, you can have them," I told him.

My neighbor slit the snake open with a knife and then cut off its head. He cut off the rattles, put them in his pocket, and walked down the road. I told Scott about the snake when he got home from school. Of course, Scott wanted to see it, so I took him down by the road. When Scott stepped on the snake's body, it popped him even though its head had been cut off! There was a bloody mess all over his boot.

"Good grief," Scott said. "Can you believe that?"

"Yeah, I can believe it," I said. "That's the only thing that snake is designed to do—strike you!"

Several years later, Phil and I went back to his house after a fishing trip. He saw a copperhead sitting on the front steps and killed it with a hoe. Phil chopped the snake into about ten pieces. Well, Jesse, who was Miss Kay's prized rat terrier dog, grabbed the snake's head and took off running. When the dog grabbed the snake's head, it struck him. The dog staggered off into the woods, and when it came back its head was swollen like a basketball! Somehow, Jesse survived the snakebite.

After I left the military, I wasn't really sure what I was going to do for the rest of my life. I was receiving a military pension, but I needed to find something to keep me busy. So I started working as a groundskeeper at a golf course near our house. Hey, there were snakes all over the golf course! One of the guys who worked with me killed a huge cottonmouth and was chasing everybody with it. When he started coming my way, I grabbed an iron stake. One of the other guys told him, "Hey, he will hurt you."

"What are you talking about?" the guy asked.

"Hey, he will wrap that iron stake around your head," the other guy said.

"The snake is already dead," he said.

"Hey, if you bring that snake any closer, you're going to be dead with him!" I said.

While I worked at the golf course, I nearly drove the superintendent slap insane because I kept asking him if I could fish for crappie in the ponds.

"You can't fish on the course!" he told me. "We have golfers out there."

"Hey, I'm not going to bother the golfers," I said. "When they come up to the green, I'll walk away and they won't even see me."

One day, the superintendent finally relented and let me fish in the ponds. I caught so many fish that I filled up the back of a golf cart cargo bed with bass and crappie. Some of the bass weighed between five and seven pounds! I must have caught thirty crappie, and they weighed about two pounds each.

The superintendent drove by me while I was fishing. "Good grief!" he said. "Where did you catch all those fish?"

"Duh," I said. "In the pond! It's a gold mine!"

After that day, the superintendent knew he wasn't going to keep me from fishing in the ponds. Before too long, I was also begging the superintendent to let me hunt deer on the golf course. Whenever we mowed the fairways, I kept seeing eight- and ten-point bucks! I chased the deer with my lawn mower all over the golf course.

"Look, are you going to let me hunt deer out here?" I asked the superintendent.

"No!" he said. "You can't deer hunt out here! There are golfers all over the place. You'll shoot one of them!"

"Hey, I'll be careful," I said. "Did you look at the pond on the third hole this morning? There were sixteen deer down there. This place is like the Graceland for whitetails!"

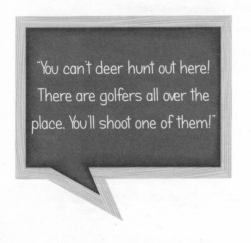

"You can't deer hunt out here! There are golfers all over the place. You'll shoot one of them!"

A few months after I quit working at the golf course, one of my buddies called me and told me he shot a sixteen-point buck on the seventeenth fairway.

"They're letting you hunt out there now?" I asked him.

"Yep, as soon as you left," he said.

I could have filled up seven freezers with venison!

I worked at the golf course for about a year, and then one of my buddies and I left to go work for Hewlett-Packard in Huntsville, Alabama. I worked in the warehouse and backed the trucks up so we could load them up with computers. I worked there for about a year, until they started talking about layoffs. Then I went to work with my neighbor, who owned a home-repair business. We remodeled houses, built decks and barns, and completed other construction projects. It was good work, but I wasn't sure I wanted to be doing manual labor for the rest of my life.

Semiretirement

One day in the winter of 1999, I called Phil to see if they were killing any ducks in Louisiana.

"Hey, when you going to come work for me?" he said. "This Duck Commander thing is really starting to take off."

"Nah, Christine told me she doesn't want to live in Louisiana," I said. "I don't think it's going to work."

"Suit yourself," Phil said. "Building duck calls is a heck of a lot more fun than repairing roofs."

Phil wasn't kidding.

"I'm so dope,
I'm illegal in fifty-five states!"

Chapter
28

Homecoming

REMEMBER WHEN I TOLD you Christine said she would never live in Louisiana again? When we were living in Alabama, I came home from work one day, and she stopped me in my tracks.

"You know what I think we should do?" she said. "If we can sell our house, we should move back to Louisiana so you can be closer to your brothers and sisters."

"Are you sick?" I asked her.

Hey, I thought Christine was terminally ill. My children and I really thought she was going to die! After we left Fort Polk near Leesville, Louisiana, she told me she would never live in the state again—no matter what! I didn't think there was any way she would ever move back to Louisiana, but she knew how much returning home meant to me. I called Trasa to tell her the news about our moving.

"Momma's dying, isn't she?" she asked.

"I think so," I said.

Christine was actually fine, but she was willing to make a sacrifice so I would be happy. I was ready to start working for Duck Commander, and Phil's business was really starting to prosper. Every time I went back to Louisiana to go hunting with Phil, he was always trying to get me to work for him. I knew Phil needed some help, and I figured helping him build duck calls would be a heck of a lot better than what I was doing for a living at the time. Christine had been working for the U.S. Department of Defense for about ten years, and she was working about ten hours a day and six days a week. We didn't have much of a life outside of work, which was really what we'd been doing our entire lives. Christine was getting ready to retire and needed a break.

Well, God must have been watching over us again. After Christine and I seriously talked about moving to Louisiana, we agreed to call a real estate agent the next Monday and advertise our house in the newspaper. Hey, we never even had to put our house on the market. We talked about it on a Friday and Saturday and went to church on Sunday morning. We told some of the people in our congregation that we were going to move to Louisiana if we could sell our house. One of the women in our church overheard us talking, and her eyes immediately lit up.

"Hey, you want to sell your house?" she said. "My daughter wants to buy it. That's her dream house."

We found out later that we had actually outbid her daughter for the house when we'd purchased it a few years earlier. I came up with a sale price that would pretty much allow us to break even or make a little bit of cash, and the lady's daughter agreed to buy it a couple of days later. There was no negotiating or haggling over the price, probably because there weren't any real estate agents involved. I probably could have asked for more money, but I was ready to move to Louisiana.

Hey, as soon as the girl signed a contract to buy my house, I packed my bags and jumped in my truck.

"Okay, baby, I'll see you later," I told Christine. "You can find me at Phil's house."

I drove straight to West Monroe and started working for Phil the next day. Well, we actually hunted and fished for a few days, but Christine doesn't need to know that. I left her behind to pack up the house and handle the details. She wasn't too happy about my leaving, but she was used to doing it, since we'd moved so many times while I was in the military. A few weeks later, Christine called me and said I had to come back to Alabama to sign the closing papers for our house.

"You can't do it without me?" I asked.

"No, honey, legally you have to be physically present to sign it," she said.

We moved to West Monroe and bought a house a few miles down the road from Miss Kay and Phil. From day one, I was the reedman at Duck Commander, which is what Phil wanted me to do. He said I made reeds better than anyone else, because nobody else took the time to do them right. Whenever Jase, Willie, Jep, or someone else built reeds, you could never build a duck call quickly because you were always fixing the reeds.

When I built the reeds, if you looked at one hundred of them, they all looked the same. They were uniform. I figured out exactly how short to cut the reeds and determined that the top reed has to be just a little bit shorter than the bottom one for the calls to sound right. After I bend two reeds and put a dimple and rivet in them so they'll stick together, you don't even have to blow the calls to make sure they sound right. Of course, Jase, Godwin, Jep, Martin, me, and other Duck Commander employees blow every duck call to make sure it sounds like an actual duck. I don't know how many reeds I've built over the years. At one point, I'd made four hundred thousand reeds, which were put into two hundred thousand duck calls. We only have one duck call that doesn't use reeds.

Of course, I didn't realize what I was getting into when I took a job with Duck Commander. I figured I'd build duck calls for a few years, and hunt and fish on most days. But when Willie bought the company from Phil, he had much bigger dreams for it. I had no idea Hollywood and cable TV were part of his plans!

They started filming me on the sly, and I never saw them doing it.

Phil had been making hunting videos for several years, and eventually I had a regular role in them. At first, whenever they pointed the cameras at me, I told them, "Hey, y'all don't have to film me. Film somebody else." I really didn't want to be on the video; I was only out there to hunt and shoot ducks. But then they started filming me on the sly, and I never saw them doing it. Jase or Willie would do something in the blind to make me angry, or I'd start telling them a story from Vietnam, and I wouldn't even know that they were filming me! Well, the people who were buying our hunting DVDs loved hearing my stories. They started calling and writing to Duck Commander, telling us they wanted to hear more Uncle Si stories.

When we went to Outdoor Channel and then A&E TV, I didn't even know how big of a role I was going to have in our shows. Willie asked me if I wanted to be involved, and I told him, "Hey, whatever y'all want me to do." Well, when A&E launched *Duck Dynasty,* I was only supposed to appear in the show occasionally. After we filmed two or three episodes of *Duck Dynasty,* they showed them to a focus group in Los Angeles. For whatever reason, the people loved watching me. They said I was the star of the show, and I wasn't even supposed to be in it! I'm not sure why I struck a nerve with so many people, but I could have never imagined people's reaction to me.

Duck Dynasty has really changed my life. It's hard to go anywhere now without being stopped for a photograph or autograph. I'm happy to do it, but nowadays it takes a lot longer to go to the gas station or grocery store. I'll do almost anything a kid asks me to do, and I know our show wouldn't be where it is today without our fans. It's amazing how many people send me free stuff at the Duck Commander warehouse. A car dealer in Arkansas even gave me a free truck to drive. The dealer put its name on the doors, and they asked me if I wanted anything else on it. I told them to put "Hey, Jack" in the back window and "The Duck Man" on the tailgate. Wouldn't you know it? I worked my entire life and never had a new truck, and now someone is giving me a free truck to drive when I'm retired.

Hey, only in America.

"One time I stopped and smelled the roses **and a big bumblebee went** and stung me on the nose. **So, hey, from then on,** look here, you smell the roses, **but you smell them quick."**

Broken Heart

ISTARTED SMOKING CIGARETTES WHEN I was in high school. Hey, back then nobody really knew that smoking was bad for you. Both of my parents smoked, and so did most of my friends' parents. All of the Hollywood actors of the 1960s smoked, whether it was Steve McQueen, Burt Lancaster, Paul Newman, or James Coburn. Hey, if those guys were smoking cigarettes, I figured it had to be cool. And, hey, there wasn't anyone cooler in Dixie, Louisiana, than Silas Merritt Robertson.

Well, I eventually figured out that a cigarette is nothing more than a pinch of tobacco rolled in paper—with fire at one end and an idiot at the other! Hey, what's the result of too much smoking? Coffin, Jack!

I smoked for more than thirty years. It was hard to quit while

I was in the military because the army gave you four cigarettes with every meal; when they stopped giving them to us, I just bought them myself. I tried to quit many times over the years. I even used tobacco alternatives like water-vapor cigarettes and electronic cigarettes. Hey, they never warned me that I could electrocute myself when I smoked them together. You want to talk about a high. Good grief!

> I eventually figured out that a cigarette is nothing more than a pinch of tobacco rolled in paper—with fire at one end and an idiot at the other!

I smoked cigarettes in Vietnam to occupy my time more than anything else. One night, a sergeant ordered a buddy and me to deliver supplies to a camp on the other side of a jungle. It was a dangerous mission, which was made even worse by a driving rainstorm. As we made our way down a dark road, I heard a tap on the passenger-side window of our Jeep.

"Hey, there's somebody knocking on my window!" I told my buddy.

"Well, open it and see what he wants," he said.

I rolled down the window. A Vietnamese man was staring at me. I didn't know if he was a civilian or with the Vietcong.

"Do you have a cigarette?" he asked.

"Hey, he wants a cigarette," I said. "What do I do?"

"Give him a cigarette and let's get out of here!" my buddy said.

I handed the man a cigarette and rolled up the window.

"Step on it," I said.

I was a little freaked out by the incident, so I lit up a cigarette of my own. Now we were really in a hurry to finish the mission, and I figured we were probably driving sixty miles per hour through the jungle. Then I heard another knock on my window.

"Good grief," I said. "He's knocking on my window again."

"Well, see what he wants," my buddy said.

I rolled down the window again.

"Do you have a light?" the Vietnamese man said.

"Light his cigarette!" my buddy said. "Make it quick!"

I lit the man's cigarette, and my buddy put the Jeep's gas pedal to the floor. We were probably going ninety miles per hour now!

Then I heard a knock on my window again.

"What in the world?" I screamed. "He's back! How is he doing it?"

I rolled down the window again, expecting him to shoot me.

"What do you want?" I asked.

"Hey, would you like some help getting out of the mud?" he said.

After I left Vietnam and quit drinking alcohol, I figured smoking wasn't the worst vice for me. I never really noticed the toll smoking was taking on my body. Even though I was smoking Winston cigarettes, I was still able to complete the mandatory training runs and any other kind of physical activity the army required of me. I even smoked when I played high school football, although the coaches probably would have killed me if they'd ever found out.

I didn't realize secondhand smoke was bad for you until I went deer hunting when I was in my forties. I was hunting on a friend's property in Germany, and he walked me to a deer stand at the start of the hunt. I climbed into the stand and lit a cigarette. A few seconds later, I heard someone coughing. I looked around for my buddy, figuring he'd come back to tell me something. But then I looked down and saw a spike buck standing next to the tree. It was coughing from the cigarette smoke! Who knew secondhand smoke was even bad for deer?

Well, eventually the cigarettes caught up with me. Near the beginning of January 2005, I knew something was wrong with my health. I was eating antacids constantly, even though my stomach was never upset by anything I ate. Growing up in Louisiana, everything we ate was spicy. I put hot sauce and pepper sauce on nearly everything—even my Fruity Pebbles. I had a cast-iron stomach. When I started feeling ill, I thought I was having heartburn or acid reflux, but the antacids weren't helping. Christine kept telling me I needed to go see the doctor, but duck season was almost over, so I wanted to keep hunting. I kept putting off a doctor's visit.

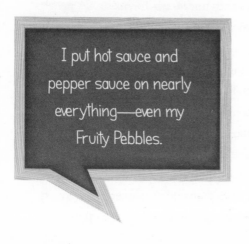

I put hot sauce and pepper sauce on nearly everything—even my Fruity Pebbles.

Christine knew I absolutely hated going to the doctor or visiting a hospital. Whenever Christine had surgery over the years, I tried to visit her, but she knew how anxious it made me. She always sent me home because I made her nervous. I visited her as soon as the surgery was over, and then I went back to get her when she was released. I figured it was the least I could do for her. It's not that I hate visiting doctors or going to the hospital, it's really more of a deeply rooted phobia. When we were kids, a mobile doctor's clinic visited the rural areas of Louisiana. Momma always took us to the clinic to get tetanus shots and other vaccinations we needed for school. Well, the first time Momma took me, I took off running through a cornfield! I don't like needles and I don't like shots, Jack!

Well, on the next-to-last day of duck season in 2005, we were sitting in a blind and killed about four or five ducks. Jase noticed a big flock of ducks flying to another part of Phil's land. They decided to pick up a few decoys and move to the other spot.

"Hey, y'all go ahead," I said. "I ain't feeling too good. I'm going to sit here and see if I can get me a couple more ducks. Y'all come back when you're done hunting."

After they left, I saw a mallard drake and mallard hen fly into the woods. I decided I was going to slip into the woods and whack 'em. I killed the mallard drake and retrieved it, but then my chest started hurting as I walked back to the blind. Suddenly, I was overcome with severe chest pains. I sat on a log and tried to catch my breath. When the pain finally abated, I walked back to my truck and drove home. I went straight to bed. I was absolutely exhausted and slept all day.

Throughout the night, Christine kept checking on me to make sure I was still breathing. She feared something was seriously wrong with me. I got up at four o'clock the next morning to go duck hunting again. When I leaned over to put on my boots, the pain in my chest took my breath away. I woke up Christine and told her I needed to go to the emergency room. She knew something was very wrong. After the nurses checked my vital signs, they admitted me to the hospital.

The doctors sent a camera scope down my throat to look at

my heart. They told me I was having a heart attack and needed open-heart surgery. Hey, I told you I was a heartbreaker!

"Are you sure I need it?" I asked the surgeon.

"Yeah, you need it," he said. "You'll die if you don't."

"Well, I've been healthy all of my life," I said. "If you say I need it, then I guess I need it."

Since it was a Saturday, the heart surgeon decided to wait to do my surgery until his regular team was on duty on Monday. I kept having heart attacks, but the doctors and nurses were monitoring me around the clock. They took really good care of me. On Monday, I had open-heart surgery. When the surgery was over, doctors told Christine that overall I was pretty healthy. They took a vein from my leg and used it to bypass a blockage and get blood to my heart. After I woke up, the surgeon told me it was a privilege to operate on me because he didn't have to do any work to find my heart. When the surgeon cracked me open, he couldn't find an ounce of fat. My heart was sitting right there. They didn't even have to put me on a heart-lung machine to pump my blood during surgery; the surgeons repaired my heart between beats!

I knew I was lucky to be alive. The surgeon told Christine I had what they called a "widow-maker." My left main coronary artery was almost completely blocked. Medically, the doctors told me, I should have died. A widow-maker can kill you within a matter of only ten to twenty minutes. It was another of God's miracles. Thankfully, the Lord was watching over me again and sent me to good doctors, nurses, and surgeons who saved my life.

My recovery from surgery was pretty rapid. It was around the time I usually helped Phil work on his land, which I really enjoyed doing. I liked being out in nature and loved spending time with my brother. I paced myself for six weeks and when I received the all clear from the doctors, I went back to my normal routine. I had shortness of breath and got tired easily for a while, but before too long, I was back to being regular ole Uncle Si.

After my heart attack, I never picked up another cigarette. I promised Christine, my children, and my brothers and sisters that I would never smoke again—and I haven't. My heart attack really woke me up, and now I cherish every day I'm on this earth. Before my heart attack, I hadn't been to the doctor since 1993. Now I get a checkup every six months. Sunrises and sunsets are a lot more beautiful now, and I even take time to smell the roses. Hey, I still smell them quick, because you never know when a bumblebee might sting you on the nose!

"Never insult a man's beard.
You get either thunder or lightning."

Chapter
30

Faith

Hey, I don't use the term "religious." A lot of people say they're religious, but then you watch how they act or listen to how they talk. Their actions and language say otherwise. I don't really care about the names on the front of a church building, either, because I don't believe in denominations. You're either a Christian or you're not.

My faith is pretty simple: I believe that God is the Father and his Son is Jesus Christ. I believe Jesus Christ came to this earth and became flesh for us because we have two problems. We have a sin problem and a death problem, and, hey, we can't solve either one of them. Jesus left our Father's side, came to this earth as flesh, and died on a cross for the things Silas Robertson does wrong. I deserve to be on a cross and would be guilty as charged for some of the things I've done in my life. Jesus was innocent of all charges and did not belong there, yet he willingly went there and accepted my punishment.

Hey, that's not the end of the story. A little girl watched her mother kill her father. The little girl went to church with her grandmother, and a Sunday school teacher showed her a picture of Jesus on the cross.

"Does anyone know who this is?" the teacher asked.

"I don't know his name," the little girl said. "But he didn't stay on the cross."

"What are you talking about?" the teacher asked.

"I know he didn't stay on the cross because the night my mother killed my father, he was holding me in his arms," the little girl said.

Jesus Christ dying on the cross wasn't the end of the story. They took his body down from the cross and buried him in a tomb. Before Jesus was crucified, he told everyone that if they ruined the temple—they thought he was referring to a religious temple, but he was actually talking about his body—he would raise it in three days. Three days after they hung Jesus on a cross and killed him, he fulfilled what he said. He rose from the dead and spent forty days and forty nights with five hundred people to prove his resurrection. Some people even watched his body ascend into the heavens.

It was all part of God's plan. Jesus came to earth of his free will and knew what he had to do. He paid for my sins and then ascended into the heavens. Right now, Jesus is sitting next to our heavenly Father. When I mess up, I say, "Lord, I'm sorry, I have sinned again because I'm weak." They look down at me, and Jesus turns to the Father and says, "Remember the cross. I have him covered."

Hey, my faith is what my momma and daddy raised me to believe. I watched them live it. They didn't only talk the talk, but they walked the walk that matched the talk. When people ask me where I go to church, I tell them I'm a follower of Jesus Christ. I'm a Christian. I believe that he is who he said he was. Jesus said he was God's son, and I believe him. I believe he died on the cross for me. I believe he beat the grave, and that's a promise he has given me. He said, "If you trust me, even if you die, you shall live."

Hey, if anyone has a better offer for me, in which my sins will be forgiven and I can beat the grave, I'm willing to listen. But I don't think I'll ever hear a better offer for everlasting life.

It's what I live by, and it's the great hope the Bible gives us. As Jase likes to say, the Bible is a love letter from God to mankind. In the Bible, God tells us how much He loves us and that He sent his Son to die for us. Some people have asked how Jesus was able to live on this earth and not sin. Some people claim Jesus really wasn't a man. Hey, Jesus was a man. He proved it to the Apostle Thomas, who doubted Jesus was resurrected until he could see and feel the wounds Jesus received on the cross.

As it says in John 20:24–29:

> Now Thomas (also known as Didymus), one of the Twelve, was not with the disciples when Jesus came. So the other disciples told him, "We have seen the Lord!"
>
> But he said to them, "Unless I see the nail marks in his hands and put my finger where the nails were, and put my hand into his side, I will not believe."
>
> A week later his disciples were in the house again, and Thomas was with them. Though the doors were locked, Jesus came and stood among them and said, "Peace be

with you!" Then he said to Thomas, "Put your finger here;
see my hands. Reach out your hand and put it into my
side. Stop doubting and believe."

Thomas said to him, "My Lord and my God!"

Then Jesus told him, "Because you have seen me, you
have believed; blessed are those who have not seen and yet
have believed."

Thomas believed Jesus was the Father's Son because he could touch and feel his wounds. Jesus was of flesh and blood, but he was also deity. If he wasn't, he couldn't help me because he wouldn't be able to understand. Jesus died on the cross because he loved perfectly. When Jesus was in excruciating pain and was dying on the cross, he told the Father, "Forgive them. They don't know what they're doing." There isn't a more painful way for a human to die than being crucified on the cross, but Jesus still forgave those who killed him.

Hey, if you're a Christian, racism is out. God made mankind from dust and then He made woman. We don't even know what color Adam was. When I was growing up in Dixie, Louisiana, there were probably only six or seven white kids in the entire town. Most of my friends were African-American. If I had chores to do, I'd get my friends to help me paint a fence, clean the barn, or cut the grass. Then I'd take them to the water hole and teach them how to swim. I probably taught twenty African-American kids how to swim.

When Daddy fell from an oil rig and broke his back, we didn't have very much money because he wasn't working. Momma told some of the ladies in the neighborhood that we weren't going to have a Christmas that year because she didn't have any money to

buy us presents. Well, the black families in town took up a dona-
tion and raised about two hundred dollars for us. We had a mem-
orable Christmas because of their generosity, and nobody even
asked them to do it. The Bible tells us to love everyone, regardless
of race or religion.

Hey, I believe in Jesus Christ and he is God's Son. He came to
this earth as flesh and died on a cross for our sins. He loved us
enough to die for us, even his enemies.

That's a fact, Jack!

Afterword

Letters to Si
from His Family

A Letter to Si from His Wife, Christine

*When I first met you, I knew you as "Rob." In the
military, names were usually shortened, and the first
name was never used. We had been together sixteen
months when I was introduced to your siblings, their
children, and your parents They called you "Si," not
"Rob," so I did the same when we were with your family.
But when we were alone, it was back to "Rob." But after
you became a household name, I decided I might as well
join the crowd.*

*When I met your family that first time, I wanted to
run in the opposite direction. You know how shy I am
and that I don't open up to people easily. It has always*

surprised me that you and I were able to talk as easily as we did from the very beginning.

You wanted to live near Phil, so we stayed with Phil, Kay, and Alan until we found an apartment not far from them. I understood that you had missed the hunting and fishing with Phil, but every time you went out with him, I worried. He was drinking by then, and I didn't trust him. After about a year, you realized he was beyond your help, and we moved to Ruston, Louisiana. I knew how that hurt your heart, but I was concerned about you. When you reenlisted in the Army, I thought it was a great idea. Even though you are strong (and stubborn), I worried about Phil rubbing off you.

Do you remember the first year you were able to duck hunt in 1971? You and Phil had killed eight, but when you cleaned them, there were only seven. Jason was now three. When he came out of the bedroom the next morning, he had the duck under his arm. Evidently he had slept with it. Phil said, "There is a duck hunter in the making!" Look at Jason now!! Alan, at such a young age, told everyone he would be a minister when he grew up. And that's exactly what he did.

When we couldn't have children, you had so much faith! In my heart, I never believed I was worthy of children. But when I became pregnant, I knew it was a special gift from God. I was only sick twice, and everything went fine. When my contractions started and were coming every fifteen minutes, you took me to the clinic. After the exam, they told you to get me straight to the hospital. It usually takes forty minutes;

*you got me there in twenty. All the way there, you kept
me laughing. When we were waiting for a nurse to
open the door, I was still laughing. When she opened
the door, she said we didn't belong there. Both of us
were shocked! She finally said, "No one who rings this
bell is laughing."*

*This was in the time before ultrasounds, so I had
to have an X-ray. I ended up having an emergency
C-section. You were there when I woke, but the only
question you were able to answer was "What was the
sex?" I wanted to know how much she weighed, how
long she was, and what color was her hair was. You
are such an observant person. NOT!! Trasa was born
on Saturday night, but you were in the midst of a huge
inspection, so you had to return to base. I'm a military
wife, and I understood that spouses have to do some
things alone. You were allowed to return to the hospital
to sign some papers; then you had to return to base.
Trasa and I were discharged on Friday, but you were
not allowed to come get us.*

*Our home was always full of love and laughter, but
with the addition of our beautiful daughter, it was even
more so.*

*Mom had always told me to be careful how I
worded prayer. When we prayed for patience, we had no
idea how God would answer. You always say that God
has a sense of humor. We sure learned patience when
we had our son. Due to complications in my pregnancy
with Scott, our family was split up. Trasa was sent to my
parents in Kentucky, you were at Fort Polk, and I was in*

Texas. We had so many people praying for us from three different states.

In our time together, we have seen God's work in so many ways. Before I knew you, my dad was the only man I loved and respected. Girls often marry men like their dads. God was first in Dad's life. He also loved Mom and didn't care who knew it. I have been so blessed by having you in my life. Because of you, I have reached the brass ring! Life with you has never been boring or mundane.

May God continue to keep you in the palm of His hand. I love everything about you and would never change anything. I'm also proud that you are now sharing your laughter and love of God with many, many people. You are awesome!

A Letter to Si from His Daughter, Trasa

When I think of you, the first word that springs to mind is "faith." You have always been so committed to God and the Church, and that definitely rubbed off on me. The years of attending church three times weekly never seemed a burden, because you made sure we knew it was the right thing to do. I learned Scripture, first by hearing it from you and then by reading it on my own. I learned so much from God's Word. I used to wake up early some mornings and memorize pieces like the Sermon on the Mount so I could be an educated Christian. That habit has continued into my adult life, and I often turn to the Bible in times of trouble and of thanksgiving. That basis, that rock, which you gave me during my childhood, has led me to be the strong Christian woman I am today.

The second word about you that wells up is "nature." You love the outdoors and all the natural gifts the world has to offer. Because of your family's background, hunting and fishing are like breathing to you. But many were the times that we would sit together and you would point out the wildlife all around us—a bunny rabbit there, here a hawk with talons extended to catch a meal, sometimes a deer as its eyes reflected green in the passing headlights. I enjoyed those times immensely as you shared your wisdom about nature.

Of course, I couldn't forget to thank you for my great love of food! As anyone who knows me will attest, I am an eater. And I'm not one of those dainty, waifish girls, either—despite my history of modeling. On our first official date, when my future husband Kyle asked me if he could cook me dinner, he asked what I'd like. He expected me to say, "Oh, a salad," or "Whatever you'd like to make." Instead, I definitively stated, "I'd love a steak and a baked potato." That part of me surely comes straight from you—as well as my love for all kinds of meats. Yep, I'm quite the carnivore. As I told a friend recently, squirrel is still the best meat I've ever eaten— but the stinkin' critters are just too small! It takes a dozen just to feed two people!

Seriously, though, a lot of my political perceptions were formed at your knee. I still believe in gun rights for hunters and also for constitutional guarantees against governmental recklessness. I believe that people are more important than things or animals. And I believe that the right to life is sacred, from conception to natural death.

Thank you for helping form me into the person I've become. I am a physically confident, emotionally mature, intellectually gifted human being, and am so blessed by God in this life with my adoring husband and beautiful sons. I could not be happier in my life.

I love you, Dad.

A Letter to Si from His Son, Scott

When I think back to my childhood, I have so many memories. I remember watching you and Trasa clean squirrels and helping y'all once I got big enough. I remember you dressing up in costumes like the big rabbit. I remember you taking me deer hunting with you in Germany. I must have driven you crazy that day with all my fidgeting. You so wanted me to get a deer and maybe share that experience of your childhood. I simply loved the fact that I got to spend a day with my dad. I watched you and listened to you more than you knew. I picked up your love of the land and being in the woods simply from watching how you moved and the different trees you pointed out.

I remember when you took me along on the wild boar hunt in Germany. I found out later I was going to be a beater, and not with you. So there I was crawling around this thick brush on the side of a mountain making a lot of noise (which I have to say I enjoyed) to drive the animal toward the hunters. The gentleman with me had a pistol, which got me thinking, What happens if the boar doesn't beat it like he's supposed to? The gentleman with the pistol said I shouldn't worry about that, as it's very rare that the boars come at the beaters. I have to say I was not very reassured. When we finally got to stand up, I was relieved, only to find that, after walking a short distance, we had to do it again at a different location.

I remember you taking me with you for your duck

hunting vacation in Louisiana when I was in the fifth grade, and fishing at night with cane poles and a lantern on the Ouachita River.

I remember when we took a family trip to Bavaria and Mom and Trasa got lost. You remained quite calm, in spite of all my questions of "What if?" I remember you reviewing the short sermon that I gave at the church we attended in Pirmasens and helping me get over my first-time jitters.

I look back at the conversations we had when I was a hardheaded teenager. I remember the heated discussions we had where you were just trying to steer me in the right direction, maybe away from mistakes you made. I remember that you wanted me to go to college, and I wanted to join the military. I thought I had my points all lined up for the discussion and that you would understand. Needless to say, the conversation didn't quite go as I'd planned, and we agreed to disagree. I can't describe to you how I felt when I came back from AIT as a soldier, and you told me that I had made the right choice. I remember you telling me that the only things I can control—something I came into this world with and will leave with—is the value of my word.

Dad, there are so many things I remember, and you are threaded through them all. I remember you telling me how much smarter your father got as you got older. I have to say I never thought you didn't know what you were talking about, though I can't say I understood as a child what I understand now as a parent myself. I look back to your words then and find myself applying them now when I hit a bump in the road of life. I have to say I am amazed at the level of patience you possessed then and now. I consider myself blessed that I had the parents I did. No one is perfect, but y'all are the perfect ones for me.

You are and always have been the rock this family holds to. Your faith in God as I grew up showed me that we might not always have the answers and that was okay, because God was in charge and would always take care of us. I love you, Dad, and will consider myself lucky if I grow up to be half the man you are.

Blessed is the man who does not walk in the counsel of the wicked or stand in the way of the sinners or sit in the seat of mockers. But his Delight is in the law of the Lord, and on his law he meditates day and night. He is like a tree planted by streams of water, which yields its fruit in season and whose leaf does not whither. Whatever he does prospers.—Psalms 1:1–3

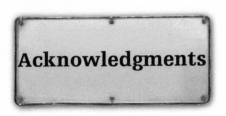

Acknowledgments

THANKS TO MY MOM and dad for raising me and introducing me to Jesus Christ and for encouraging my love for hunting and fishing. Thanks to Mark Schlabach for taking my stories and putting them all together to show my journey so far. Thanks to Philis Boultinghouse, Amanda Demastus, and our friends at Howard Books. Thanks to Phil and Kay and their family for being there for all of my life. Thanks to Alan for helping with the book. Thanks to John Howard for his help. Thanks to my poker buddies for keeping me sane. Thanks to Trasa, Kyle, Scott, and Marsha for making me proud and giving me eight wonderful grandsons. Finally, thanks to my wife, Christine, that redhead who has kept life interesting for the past forty-three years.

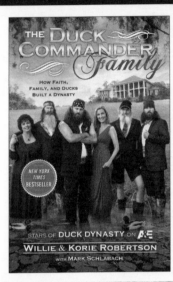